A CHINA STORY

RECOGNITIONS

2026 Feathered Quill Book Awards
Bronze Award for Memoir/Biography

2025 Reviewers Choice Awards
Gold Award for Classics
Memoir/Autobiography/Biography

2025 Memoir Prize for Books
Category Winner Award for History/Culture

2020 North Street Book Prize
Honorable Mention Award for Creative Nonfiction
(Advance Reader Copy)

2019 BookLife Prize
Quarter Finalist for Memoir/Autobiography
(Manuscript)

"Qian excels at viscerally recreating Mao's China as filtered through her childhood perceptions, while supplying readers with edifying historical context. ... Qian's memoir offers a highly effective framing device, which also allows the work to stand apart from other titles that unfold during the years of the Cultural Revolution. Qian's story—of her family, her father, and her own journey from Beijing to the United States and back—is a unique and memorable one."

—BookLife Prize

"A woman takes us back through time in her riveting story about growing up in Mao's Communist China. The aftereffects and revelation of what really happened to her father are astounding. This story is powerful and worth reading. Honest and eye-opening."

—San Francisco Book Review

"A beautifully and bravely written masterpiece, survivor Ying Qian's historical account of growing up during the Mao-mandated Cultural Revolution keeps readers riveted as it tugs at the heartstrings and exposes unspeakable horrors that have been swept under the rug for far too long."

—Christine Pingleton

Writer, Editor, Founder of Word Works Editorial Service

A CHINA STORY

Growing Up in Mao's
Cultural Revolution

An Award-Winning Memoir

YING QIAN

Published by Opening Line Publishing

ISBN 978-0-578-66179-7

Disclaimer

To protect individuals and their privacy, some names in this book have been changed.

For more information: www.achinastory.com

To my parents

CONTENTS

The Great Proletarian Cultural Revolution officially started on May 16, 1966, when the Communist Party published the May 16 Notification, which was seen as the manual of the great purge. But to me, it started the day my elderly neighbors crawled on the ground like dogs, their eyes filled with fear and sweat dripping down their wrinkled faces.

CHAPTER ONE

When I stepped out of the airport in the late morning, the hot summer sun was beaming down from the cloudless sky above Beijing.

On the long ride into the city from the airport, the taxi driver pointed out the new skyscrapers that towered over the broad streets and crawling traffic. The capital city had just hosted the Olympics two years before, and the architectural marvels were proud evidence of the dazzling event. "You have to see the buildings up close," the man said under his faded blue cap. "You must," he pressed.

I was silent.

Beijing was more than a city where ancient palaces commanded admiration and new high-rises aroused national pride. Beijing was my hometown, a place where I had spent the first 30 years of my life, a place where a Persian silk tree's pink flowers and tender green leaves swayed in front of Mother's apartment window and my grandparents' soft old Beijing dialect lingered behind their courtyard walls, a place where I had learned my first songs and made my first friends. Beijing was also a place where my world had collapsed and my heart had been broken, a place I had turned my back on 22 years earlier when I left China for America.

Like all other trips back to China, I had planned to spend quiet time with my family: short, peaceful, and pleasant, the way a dragonfly quickly touches the surface of the water and takes off. I feared that any prolonged stay or extensive conversations might trigger painful memories and open deep wounds.

I checked into a hotel near Mother's apartment before noon. The walls of the small hotel room were covered with dated yellowish wallpaper. On one side, a queen bed lay below a window. On the other side, against the wall, stood a brown wardrobe. A small table with a glass top was pushed against the wall near the door. I put away my luggage and sat down on a wooden chair by the table.

I heard a knock at the door; it was my older brother and his wife.

"Your sister-in-law made some dumplings for you to snack on," my brother said, handing over a plastic container before sitting down on a chair by the closet. Under a white cap, his face was red from walking in the summer heat.

I curbed my desire to hug him. We hadn't grown up hugging each other. We Chinese preferred to show our affection in tangible ways, not through words or hugs.

My sister-in-law, in her tailored light-colored shirt and trousers, sat at the edge of the bed. She took out a handkerchief from a black tote bag and fanned herself with it.

I called my sister-in-law by her name, Feng, but called my brother Big Brother because he was the oldest of the three siblings. It was common for a Chinese person to address older siblings based on their birth order: Big Brother, Second Brother, etc.

"Come and eat with me," I said, opening the container and turning to Feng.

She didn't answer me. Instead, she looked at Big Brother and asked, "Should we tell her?"

He nodded without looking at either his wife or me. Feng turned to me. Her lips started to tremble, and her eyes welled up. I was alarmed.

"Your brother and I just found out how your father died," she said. Her face was getting red.

I felt as if someone had punched me in the chest. I sat down on a chair by the table and took a deep breath. Feng was choking up. Her shoulders heaved. She covered her face with her hands and cried.

Big Brother stared at the window, stone-faced.

My father had died 40 years before. He'd been a nuclear weapons expert and had been killed by the Chinese military during the Great Proletarian Cultural Revolution, a witch hunt launched by the leader of the Chinese Communist Party, Mao Zedong, in 1966, when I was eight years old.

A dictator, Mao had ruled China by fear. To strengthen his control and cleanse the country of his foes, he'd launched numerous political movements during the 27 years he'd ruled China. The longest and the deadliest was the Cultural Revolution. The 10-year purge had turned the nation into a jungle and people into prey. Countless people had suffered, and hundreds of thousands, if not millions, had died. Father was one of them.

The government had never attempted to catch the killers, and our family had never learned the details of Father's death because we'd never had access to the autopsy report.

In a way, I preferred not knowing how he had died. The fact that it had been during a military interrogation was difficult enough for everyone in my family. More details would only cause more pain.

Feng wiped her eyes and took out a few pages from her bag. They were a copy of an article from the March 2007 issue of a Chinese-language magazine, *Ordnance Knowledge*. "The article tells what a horrific death your father had," she said, handing me the copy. "I will let you read it yourself."

I took the copy but didn't read it.

I folded up the pages carefully, making sure the words were inside so that I wouldn't see them accidentally. I put the article in my suitcase and then put the suitcase back in the closet.

"Don't tell Mother what's in the article," Feng said before she and Big Brother left.

CHAPTER TWO

1966

The soft morning sun shone through the three large, east-facing windows in our classroom, lending a hint of pink color to Teacher Li's face. A portrait of Mao sat high above the blackboard behind her.

Thin and pale, Teacher Li was in her mid-thirties. Her straight pitch-black hair rose in the front like a tiara before it gently folded back on her shoulders. The mandarin collar of her dark blue shirt hugged her long neck.

She read to us an editorial in the state-run newspaper *People's Daily*: "We will carry on a long-term struggle against bourgeois and petty-bourgeois thoughts."

I was eight years old and in my second year in elementary school. The Cultural Revolution had just started, but I had already heard the rumors that some young people had been cutting up people's clothes on the streets of Beijing if they considered them evidence of a decadent lifestyle: shirts too tight, skirts too short, or pants with bell-bottoms. I was scared by what I had heard.

Teacher Li continued reading. I didn't quite understand all the complicated words in the article: "bourgeois class," "representatives of the bourgeois class," "class struggle," etc. However, I could see the excitement on Teacher Li's face. She raised her voice as she read, "Our nation is facing a great climax of the Great Proletarian Cultural Revolution."

After she had finished reading, Teacher Li held the sides of the chest-high yellow podium with both hands, and her upper body leaned forward toward her students. She asked us, "Who will answer our great leader Chairman Mao's calling and carry out the Cultural Revolution to the end?" She smiled, her eyes sparkling.

"We will!" we shouted out together.

Seeing Teacher Li's enthusiasm toward the Cultural Revolution, I knew I should support the political movement. I always listened to my teacher. I trusted her.

I met Teacher Li on my first day of elementary school. Mother was a chemistry teacher at the university where our family lived. She had to teach that day and couldn't walk me to school.

Father couldn't either. As far as I could remember, he

had never lived with us. Mother told me that Father used to teach chemistry at the same university where she worked. When I was two, the government sent him away to the Qinghai-Tibet Plateau, more than a thousand miles west of Beijing, to work at an institute code-named Factory 221. I didn't know the nature of Father's work until after his death. Our family—Mother, my two brothers, and I—continued living on the university campus where Mother worked. We only saw Father during his annual visits back to Beijing.

The morning of my first day of school, I made my hair into two short braids dangling by my ears and put on a white shirt and my favorite pink skirt with white polka dots. Mother put a brand-new brown school bag on my shoulder and said to me, "Obey the teachers." With Father away, Mother had been the authority figure in my life; now she had told me to obey someone else. It made me realize that now I had an authority even higher than Mother: my teachers.

On the first floor in a plain, four-story gray brick school building, I found my name on a new student list on a door. I tiptoed into the room and sat in an empty seat behind a heavy wooden desk. Teacher Li stood in front of the class, wearing a button-down lavender shirt. Her face was pale, and her skin smooth. She smiled at me.

That day, she told the class that Chinese children were the luckiest children in the world and the flowers of our motherland.

"We owe all our happiness to our great leader Chairman Mao," she said. Her face opened up.

I was mesmerized by my teacher: her smile, her eyes that filled with warmth, her beautiful words, and the bright future that she promised us.

From a very young age, I knew I was supposed to be a good child, a child of whom adults approved. Mother wanted me that way. Many years later, I realized that Mother was raising me to be like Father, who was perfect in her eyes: an intelligent person with a heart of gold. I did well in school and got along with my friends. I obeyed my teachers.

By the end of the semester, I was elected class chairman by my classmates. Teacher Li put a long slogan on the back wall of our classroom. The characters, written in black ink on white paper, read,

"Learn from Qian Ying: study hard and obey orders."

When the Cultural Revolution broke out before my first school year ended, everything changed.

Our residential area used to be monotone but orderly, with identical four-story gray brick buildings connected by concrete paths. Now the lower portion of the buildings was covered with posters. Big Chinese characters were written on the red, yellow, or green paper, condemning anything old: old city government, old school system, and old traditions. As time went by, new posters were pasted over the old ones. A thick layer of paper wrapped around the buildings like a colorful quilt.

A red banner dangled from the roof of the building facing ours. The three big black characters on the banner read: "Dou Zheng Cun," meaning "Class Struggle Village." It was the new name for the residential area. The revolutionaries had banned the old name, Happy Village, because it "covered up the class struggles."

A slogan was painted on the concrete path in front of our building in bold strokes: "Down with the biggest capitalist-roader Liu Shaoqi!" Liu's name was twisted in such a way that it read "Liu the dog." Liu Shaoqi, the chairman of China before the Cultural Revolution, used to stand next to Mao on top of Tiananmen Gate during the National Day celebrations. Now he was purged as the biggest enemy of the state for trying to bring capitalism to China, and the revolutionaries came up with every way to humiliate him. Three years later, he would die in confinement.

Old songs were banned. We were not allowed to sing my favorite song about a little rowboat floating on the lake and the cool breeze caressing children's faces anymore. Now we sang: "Big machete chops down on foreign devils' heads" or "Pick up our pen and use it as a knife or a spear."

I lost my title as class chairman because having one was part of Liu Shaoqi's educational line. Teacher Li took down the slogan that had promoted me as a role model for my classmates. When she did it, I was there to help her. She stood on a desk, took the slogan off the wall, and handed it to me. Our eyes met, but she didn't say anything. She didn't even smile. I had hoped she would at least smile at me to let me know that she hadn't taken down the slogan because she was mad at me.

The back wall was left empty until, one day, Teacher Li put up a poster of Mao's quotation in bright red characters: "You should care about national affairs and carry on the Great Proletarian Cultural Revolution to the end."

Teacher Li now addressed us as "little revolutionary fellows" instead of "the flowers of the motherland." Flowers and birds were considered symbols of the bourgeois during the Cultural Revolution. She also stopped wearing the pastel-colored shirts that I liked very much. Instead, she now wore either blue or gray shirts because drab colors were considered proletarian and, therefore, revolutionary.

The only thing that had not changed was her hairstyle. It still rose above her face in the front like a tiara, unlike other teachers whose plain hair lay flat on their heads.

I played with my friends on the wide asphalt roads of the university campus every day during the summer break, jumping rope or playing hopscotch. Often, as we played, two or three pedal-powered flatbed tricycles would zoom by, one behind another, with a bunch of young people sitting on them. They wore distinctive outfits: faded yellowish-green military uniforms, military hats, and brown leather belts as wide as my palm that cinched their waists. Their legs dangled on the sides of the tricycles as they shouted out Mao's quotations through bullhorns: "Marxism boils down to one sentence: 'Rebellion is justified!'" or "Don't ever forget class struggle!"

They were the Red Guards, college students who were Mao's loyalists. Instead of going home, they stayed on campus during the summer break to participate in the Cultural Revolution. They had red armbands on their upper-left arms. On the armband, three yellow Chinese characters in Mao's wild handwriting read: "The Red Guards." Although they were loud and brisk, I hadn't seen them hurt people—yet.

The revolutionaries had installed loudspeakers on the roofs of the buildings, and Mao's quotations or editorials from the newspapers were blared out all the time.

From the loudspeakers, I learned that on August 18, 1966, Mao had stood up high on top of Tiananmen Gate and received the adulation of one million revolutionaries. "Our great leader Chairman Mao walked up Tiananmen Gate with vigorous strides, and his face was in the pink of health, glowing with radiating vitality," a loud male voice read an editorial from *People's Daily* with exaggerated excitement. The same voice told us that Mao had a Red Guard's red armband on his left arm and that he had said to the female Red Guard who had given him the armband, "Be violent."

Having never dreamed our great leader would promote violence, I interpreted Mao's comment to be his way of encouraging the girl to be brave and powerful, not to be like "a flower growing in a greenhouse," as the bourgeoisie was often portrayed. However, the phrase "Be violent" became the Red Guards' guideline of action. Mao's support for the Red Guards set the nation on fire.

One morning soon after Mao's Tiananmen Gate appearance, I woke up to a loud noise. It was the milkwoman who used to deliver milk in glass jars to people's doorsteps every morning. Once a month, carrying a large bronze gong, she would walk around the apartment buildings and collect milk money. She would bang her gong and shout, "Milk money is due now." I was surprised to hear the milkwoman because the Red Guards had forbidden her from delivering milk. Having milk delivered was bourgeois, according to the Red Guards.

I got up and looked out the window. The milkwoman had turned the corner. The bright sunshine indicated another hot day. There was no one outside. The concrete road lay empty in front of our building.

A few minutes later, she reappeared, walking toward our apartment building. She had a gong larger than a washbasin in her left hand and a mallet wrapped in a piece of red cloth in her right. I stepped on a small chair and opened the window. The gentle, sweet summer air flowed in, along with the scream of the woman, "Landlords, come downstairs right now." Her screeching voice pierced through the tranquil morning and bounced between the apartment buildings.

Landlords were the people who owned farmland before the communists took over China in 1949, nine years before I was born. I had learned in the movies and at school that they were the people's enemies because they exploited poor peasants.

Mother walked in and stood next to me. Wearing her ivory-colored short-sleeved shirt and wide-legged pants made of soft cotton, she came as quietly as a summer breeze. Her soft black hair gently framed her oval face. Looking out the window, she frowned and tightened her lips. I sensed something unusual was about to happen.

The milkwoman walked away, clanging her gong. A few Red Guards showed up outside our apartment building.

A gray-haired woman, known as Twins' Grandma, came out from her apartment, which faced ours. She paused when she saw the Red Guards but then continued walking toward our building. A little farther away, more landlords, most of them elderly women with bound feet—a result of the common practice of foot-binding that ended in the early 20th century—shuffled toward our building under the Red Guards' escort. Before long, there were approximately two dozen landlords gathered outside our window.

Aunt Yang, our neighbor's live-in maid, came out from our building and stood in the crowd of landlords. She was in her fifties, with straight salt-and-pepper hair that touched her shoulders. She was not my relative. It was a Chinese custom for a child to call an adult woman "Aunt" or "Grandma" even if she was not a relative. Aunt Yang was my favorite grown-up in our building. Each time she saw me, she called me Da Ying, meaning "Big Ying." It always made me laugh because I was eight years old and other adults called me Xiao Ying, which means "Little Ying."

I was surprised to discover that the elderly were class enemies. I saw them on campus all the time, getting some sunshine or playing with their grandchildren. They looked nothing like the mean landlords I saw in the movies: Zhou, the meanie, who crowed like a rooster at midnight to wake up his farmhands so that they could start their workday early, or Nan, the bully, who often beat his maid into unconsciousness.

The Red Guards rounded up the former landlords, walked them eastward, and turned the corner.

Some onlookers, most of them children and teenagers, had gathered in front of our building.

The milkwoman was coming around with her gong again. When she got closer, I heard her screaming, "Professors, come downstairs right now!"

I almost fell off my chair. *Are professors bad people, too?* I wondered. At school, we were told that landlords were class enemies, but never the professors.

The professors filed out of the apartment buildings and gathered in front of our window. A slim man with gray hair came out of our building first. A math professor who lived across the hallway from us followed.

Mother didn't go down because she was a lecturer and wouldn't become a professor until the Cultural Revolution was over.

The Red Guards made the professors kneel on the concrete pavement, facing away from the building. I watched in disbelief. These were the people I called "Uncle" or "Grandpa." They had known me since I was born and watched me grow. Now they were kneeling there, being humiliated.

The Red Guards pinned a big white cloth on the back of each professor and wrote on it with black ink. I couldn't tell from where I stood what they were writing, but from that day on, I saw some people walking around campus with big white cloths on their backs. Written on the white cloths were the nicknames the Red Guards had created for the professors: Giant Poison Snake Wang, Old Cunning Fox Xu, and so forth.

Kneeling between two men was a middle-aged woman with dark-framed glasses. A male Red Guard in yellowish-green baggy unisex clothes shaved off the woman's shoulder-length hair from the right-hand side of her head, leaving the left-hand side untouched. I had heard of this creation of the Red Guards. They called the hairstyle "Yin-Yang head" because, after it was done, the head looked half black with hair and half white with bare skin, like the yin and yang symbol. As laughter burst from the crowd, the woman's hair fell from her head like a tree shedding its autumn leaves.

I watched it all, hands on the windowsill and nose pressed against the window screen. It was a heartbreaking scene. Before this day, I hadn't known that human beings could treat others so cruelly.

Teacher Li told us as soon as we entered elementary school that we should respect our teachers as if they were our fathers. It was a Chinese tradition, according to her. The college students must have known it, too. People had changed so fast; it scared me.

I was too young to know that people hadn't changed. Their behavior had. The mob behavior displayed in front of me was descended from the herd mentality that was still deeply seated in all of us. People act human in a normal society, but when allowed or even encouraged, some will act like pack animals.

As I looked at the triumphant Red Guards and the complying professors outside our window, fear crept into my heart. It was a fear of my fellow human beings, especially the misguided, self-righteous mobs, although I was too young to articulate it at the time.

More people rushed over from every apartment building as if a circus had come to town. As the crowd grew thicker, it was getting more difficult for me to see what the Red Guards were doing to the professors, but I could hear cheers breaking out from the crowd.

When I heard chaotic footsteps running up the stairs, my heart started pounding.

Just a few days before, three Red Guards had come to our home.

"Why don't you have our great leader Chairman Mao's portraits on the walls?" a female Red Guard had barked as she'd strutted about in Mother's room. The young woman's face had been red with anger. A green military cap had covered the back of her head. She hadn't looked at us. Instead, she'd screamed into the air as if we were invisible. As rude as the Red Guards had been, they hadn't touched anyone at that time. Now they seemed much more aggressive.

Mother walked across the hallway and into my teenage brothers' room, but it was empty. They must have sneaked out earlier. It was just Mother and me. We stood in the hallway behind the apartment door, waiting for that dreaded knock. I held Mother's hand and stared at the latch on the door, fighting the urge to run over and latch it. I could feel my heart beating inside my chest.

Someone banged on our door. Mother opened it.

In the dim light of the dark doorway, I saw two young men standing in front of us. One was tall and thin, and the other was shorter and stockier. I assumed they were university students.

"Is there any landlord here?" the tall man asked. He didn't sound as angry as the female Red Guard who had demanded Mao's portraits on the walls, but he was intense. His shoulders were up to his ears, and he spoke fast.

"No," Mother answered.

"Is there any professor here?"

"No."

"Are you a professor?"

"No, I am not."

"What are you?"

"I am a lecturer."

"Why are you living here, then?" the tall man asked.

Our building was the first apartment building built by the university. When it was completed, the university had assigned the apartments to the professors and their families.

"My husband was an associate professor at the university before the government sent him to work in Qinghai," Mother said. "That's how we get to live here."

The man relaxed his shoulders. He led the way down the narrow hallway into Mother's room. The other man walked behind him. Mother and I followed.

Mother's room was small and narrow, with white walls and no decoration except for Mao's portrait on a wall. The south-facing window let in ample light. Most furniture in the room belonged to the university, and its colors were mismatched—some pieces were yellow, and some were brown. A desk, a dresser, and a standalone closet were lined up against a wall on the right-hand side. Across the room was a bed. When the four of us stood in the middle of the room and faced each other, I saw the shorter man had a pair of scissors in his hand. My heart beat fast again.

"We are here to help you get rid of the 'Four Olds,'" the tall student said.

From the big loudspeakers near our home, I had learned that getting rid of the Four Olds was one of the Red Guards' main tasks given by the government. The Four Olds included old ideas, old culture, old customs, and old habits.

The tall man opened the yellow closet and took out Mother's clothes one piece at a time. He looked at the front of each piece, then the back, and then tossed it on the bed. He was looking for "outlandish clothes." I had heard that term on the radio.

The shorter student joined in, too. His head, shoulders, and torso disappeared into the deep closet. Clothes piled up on the bed, and a few pieces slid down onto the floor. The shorter man came out of the closet with Mother's two-tone jacket. The front and back were gray, and the sides were dark blue.

"This is bourgeois," he said and cut it into pieces.

I looked at Mother. She didn't try to stop the students. She didn't even frown.

The sound of footsteps and people's voices came from all over the building; the Red Guards were "helping" our neighbors.

The tall Red Guard asked to see Mother's bankbook. I didn't know what the man was going to do with it, but I knew having too much money was a bad thing. At school, we were taught that money was bad and the more money one had, the more evil the person became.

Flipping through the thin little book the size of an adult's palm, the tall man frowned. "Three thousand yuan?" he asked, looking at Mother. "Is this all your savings?" He waved the bankbook in his hand. "You have to have more than just this." He raised his eyebrows.

"That's all we have," Mother said. "We have two sets of parents and three children to support." The man returned the bankbook to her. The students left without speaking another word.

Mother quickly closed the apartment door and came back to her room. Without saying anything, she started to pick up the pieces of her jacket from the concrete floor. I bent down to help her.

I didn't know how I should feel about the whole thing. I couldn't tell whether the Red Guards had been helping us, as they had said, or just being mean. I looked at Mother's face for an answer. She didn't look at me, and her lips were tense. She didn't want to talk.

Looking back now, I realize Mother's dilemma. She couldn't have said anything to me. After living in communist

China for 17 years and having survived numerous political movements, she had learned to self-censor even behind closed doors.

As I was picking up the last pieces of the jacket, I heard the milkwoman's voice again. "Associate professors come downstairs immediately." Her penetrating voice gave me chills. I didn't remember her voice ever being so abrasive in the past.

Mother stood up. Pieces of her jacket fell on the floor from her lap and her hands. She grabbed my hand and pulled me up. It was summer, but her hand was icy cold. "Quick, let's get out of here," she said. We walked downstairs. The tall man who had just been in our apartment stood by the door. He looked at us but didn't stop us. We walked out of the building and turned the corner, leaving the crowd behind us.

Across a wide street from campus lay a vineyard. Following an irrigation ditch, Mother and I walked deep into the vineyard and sat down on a ridge. No one was around; only endless rows of grapevines stood in silence under the sun. Their tender green leaves shimmered from gusts of hot wind.

"The Red Guards already have the professors and associate professors," Mother said, brushing aside the bangs that dangled in front of my eyes with her fingers. "I was afraid they were going to order the lecturers to come out of the building next."

It was the first time I had heard Mother use the word "afraid" to describe her feelings. In my mind, she was always strong and upbeat. But now she seemed vulnerable. I was scared. Before this day, I had always thought our home was the safest place.

We hid in the vineyard until it became too hot to stay. We wandered outside the campus and walked along the street, killing time. Sometimes we sat in the shade of a tree, counting passing buses.

When we got back to the campus in the late afternoon, the revolutionaries and the professors were gone. Pieces of fabric and strands of hair were scattered on the ground. Little pieces of paper swirled in the wind.

We walked back to our apartment to find that my brothers were still not home. The noise of loudspeakers came through the window. It was from an outdoor theater about 300 yards south of our home.

"It sounds like a rally," Mother said.

"I'll take a look," I said.

"No."

"I am just a child. I'll be fine."

"OK. If you see your brothers, tell them to come home immediately." She sounded stressed.

I ran to the outdoor theater, which was bordered by green hedges almost as tall as I was. A stage with a green arched roof sat at one end. A long red banner stretched across the stage, indicating that there had been an organized rally, but it was over now. Two young men were on the stage, coiling up wires and taking away microphones. The crowds remained and formed a few circles in front of the stage. Loud cheers and laughter burst out from the crowds. After pushing and shoving, I got inside one circle.

In the middle of the crowd were a few wooden benches about two feet high and no more than seven inches wide. I had seen carpenters use them to jack up boards when they cut them. Now each bench had a landlord kneeling on it. The benches were so narrow that the elderly had to kneel across them on their shin bones. Their heads were lowered. Some of them had broken woks or old helmets on their heads, and their gray hair stuck out from under them. The university students were gone, leaving neighborhood children and teenagers to continue tormenting the landlords. I looked around and didn't see my brothers.

The children and teens seemed to be more excited than during a Chinese New Year celebration. They knocked the woks with sticks and spat on the landlords. One boy looked up at a male landlord's face under a wok. "Hey, old man, are you crying?" he asked. Laughter erupted from the crowd. Not far from me was one of my classmates. The usually timid boy was now laughing hard.

The party continued until the sound of a bugle call came from the loudspeakers, signaling the opening of the campus cafeterias. It was time for dinner. The crowds started moving back to Class Struggle Village. The tormentors were walking and running, while the landlords were crawling on their hands and knees. The children and teenagers ran back and forth, laughing and screaming, waving the sticks in their hands as if they were shepherds herding sheep.

I was scared. In addition to the sound of cheering and laughing, there was a touch of nervousness in the air; it seemed the boys could barely contain their excitement.

Something even worse could happen.

I walked back toward our apartment building by myself, leaving behind the landlords and their abusers. At home, I told Mother the rally was over and I hadn't seen my brothers. I didn't tell her about the heinous scene I had seen. I wished I hadn't seen the crawling elderly and the jubilant teenagers. I would rather forget the terrible day.

The Great Proletarian Cultural Revolution officially started on May 16, 1966, when the Communist Party published the *May 16 Notification*, which was seen as the manual of the great purge. But to me, it started the day my elderly neighbors crawled on the ground like dogs, their eyes filled with fear and sweat dripping down their wrinkled faces.

At dinner that night, Mother grilled my brothers about their whereabouts during the day. A low ceiling light cast a yellowish glow down on the burgundy dining table. My brothers, in their dark blue shirts, sat still with their heads down. It turned out they had sneaked into a shooting range in a fenced, military-controlled area on campus to search for spent shell casings. There was a platoon of soldiers stationed on campus year-round for security reasons.

"Didn't I tell you not to go there?" Mother said. Her eyes stayed on their faces for a while before she turned to me. "You need to lock the door when you are home alone. Things are different now." Up to this point, we had only latched our door when we slept at night. "You only open the door when you hear your brothers' voices or my voice," Mother said. I nodded.

Mother stopped talking. The room fell into silence. I looked out the window. It was dark outside, and my reflection in the window looked back at me. Outside, the Red Guards rode flatbed, pedal-powered tricycles around the apartment buildings. Through bullhorns, they shouted, "They are a bunch of counter-revolutionaries who are anti-communist and anti-people. Our struggle against them is a struggle in which I live and you die."

What had happened during the day was like a bad dream: the crawling elderly neighbors, the kneeling professors, and the Red Guards who cut up Mother's jacket. The world was not the world that Teacher Li had described for us, where the motherland was like a giant flower garden and children were the brilliant flowers in it. The behavior I had seen was the opposite of what I had been told a good person should demonstrate. Most confusing was that as scary as the revolutionaries were, they were encouraged by the government because their revolutionary actions would make our nation stronger and people's lives better, as the government-controlled media told us. Our socialist motherland was still great despite the chaos and violence.

That night, I couldn't sleep. I missed Father. If he had been home, Mother wouldn't have been so stressed.

When I was little, whenever Father was home on his vacations, he was the one, not Mother, who told me bedtime stories. Sometimes, when I was too excited to sleep, Father would stroke the bridge of my nose between my eyebrows with his fingers, and that would make my eyelids heavy and put me to sleep.

When fall came, the new semester started. All regular classes—reading, writing, and arithmetic—were suspended by the government so that we could participate in the Cultural Revolution full time. Going to school meant reciting Mao's quotations and memorizing Mao's articles. We carried Mao's quotation book all the time. We called it the "red book of treasure" because of its red cover. Throughout the day, Teacher Li would ask us to turn to a page of the book. "Our great leader Chairman Mao teaches us," she would begin. We would then read a paragraph out loud together.

Our elementary school was part of the university, and all the students were the children of university employees. Every once in a while, our school sent its students to participate in persecution rallies against university officials. The rallies were usually held at the outdoor theater. An area was reserved in front of the stage for us elementary school students. We sat on little folding chairs that we brought from home. The university students and employees sat around or behind us.

In the rallies, university officials were forced to stand on a stage with their heads lowered, and a big board, two feet by three feet, with their names written on it hung from their necks by a wire. They received a treatment called "jet plane," where two young men held each official's arms from behind and, at the same time, pushed the officials' heads down. It was called "jet plane" because the victims resembled the shape of an airplane; the lifted arms were the wings of the aircraft. It was designed to instill both physical pain and emotional humiliation. People took turns screaming abuse at the officials through loudspeakers. From time to time, the crowd shouted slogans: "Down with capitalist-roaders!""Down with anyone who is against Chairman Mao!"

At first, the roar of the slogans startled me. When thousands of people howled together in anger, it sounded like a caged beast. The air trembled, and I could hear the rage in people's voices. *Being hated by so many people is horrible,* I thought. Gradually, the rallies became a norm. With each slogan, we raised our fists, and from the angry speeches, we learned to hate.

1967

After banning regular classes in school for more than a year, the government ordered us to "resume classes and carry out the revolution." Besides reciting Mao's work and going to rallies, we also learned arithmetic and new Chinese characters. I welcomed the changes because the more Chinese characters I learned, the better the letters I could write to Father, and at nine years old, I started reading classic novels. After school, I often immersed myself in the world of Jane Eyre or David Copperfield. It helped me escape the chaos caused by the political movement. The Chinese characters I learned made reading faster and more enjoyable. Although the government banned the classic novels and labeled them "giant poisonous weeds," the Red Guards hadn't destroyed them when they'd raided our home. I suspected that it was because the Red Guards who had come to our home were college students and had books of their own. The Red Guards who raided Father's parents' home in another part of the city were junior high or high school students. They burned all my grandparents' books except for children's books.

CHAPTER THREE

1968

It was two years into the Cultural Revolution when the government sent two military men to our school to lead the political movement. Our school was not the only one. During the next few years, more than 2,800,000 soldiers were sent to factories and schools all over China to take control of civilian life. They were called "Liberation Army Mao Zedong Thought Propaganda Teams."

The morning the military came, Teacher Li brought an armful of little red flags to our class.

"Great news!" she said, dropping the little flags on the podium in front of the blackboard. Her smooth face was glowing. "Our great leader Chairman Mao sent the people he trusts the most, the People's Liberation Army, to our school." The classroom erupted with loud cheers.

Thanks to the government's propaganda, the Chinese

people, including me, idolized the military men. Not only did the media praise the military as "a great wall of steel and iron" protecting China from the attacks of the "American Imperialists," but it also used them as a role model for the whole nation, calling them "the most lovable people" with the highest morals.

We grabbed the little red flags from the podium and filed out of the classroom to join the rest of the school in welcoming the military.

The students and teachers lined up along the road leading to the school building, waiting for the soldiers. It was cold, and the wait was long. Teacher Li stretched her neck and stuck out her chest to show us that we wouldn't be shivering if we stood up straight instead of sinking our necks into our cotton-padded jackets like turtles.

At first sight of the two soldiers walking down the road, the students raised their little red flags and shouted slogans: "Learn from the Uncle Liberation Army!" "Salute to the Uncle Liberation Army!" The official title of the military men was military representatives, but we called them the "Uncle Liberation Army."

The soldiers were fully uniformed, with green clothes, brown belts, and green sneakers. Carrying no weapons, they were young and not much taller than some of the students. I looked around and saw smiling faces. Teacher Li was smiling, too, waving a little red flag. The soldiers rushed through the crowd and disappeared into the school building.

Things were different after the military came to the school.

We still had classes in the morning, but in the afternoons, we marched. The goal of the endless marching was to train us to obey orders. Teacher Li told us that through the marching practice, we would be stronger, less bourgeois, and better suited to be "successors to the revolutionary cause of the proletariat." The school playground was not big enough for the whole school to march on. Some classes had to march on the university athletic fields. To help the two soldiers train the students, the school borrowed more military men from the platoon stationed on the university campus.

We sang Mao's quotation songs and shouted Mao's quotation while marching:

> *Make up my mind,*
> *No fear of death,*
> *Conquer 10,000 obstacles,*
> *And achieve victories!*

Mao didn't send the military just so that we could learn goose steps, though.

It is a myth that most misery and death during the Cultural Revolution was caused by the Red Guards. In fact, it occurred during the Purifying Class Ranks Movement under the military rule.

Under the soldiers' watch, the Purifying Class Ranks Movement was in full bloom in our school. Wires were stretched across the hallways in our school building, and big-character posters hung from the wires like clothes dangling from clotheslines. We had to lower our heads when we walked down the hallways. I didn't read the posters because I thought that they were written by teachers and were adults' business.

For now, the political movement meant rallies and marching practice, but the rest of my life was not greatly impacted. One day, though, it all changed.

It was a regular school day. The weather was mild, and the windows in our classroom were open to allow in the fresh air. Surrounding our four-story school building was a sprawl of rowhouses made of red bricks, which housed university staff members and their families. Once in a while, a woman's voice or a baby's cry came through the windows.

Teacher Li was wearing a blue shirt with a mandarin collar and kimono sleeves. Her face was as pale as always. She leaned against the side of the podium and held the newspaper with both hands.

There was Mao's headshot in the upper portion of the front page. When Teacher Li read the article printed below Mao's photo to us, she folded the newspaper in the middle, and as a result, Mao was now upside down.

"How could you?" someone screamed with intense urgency, like a cat whose tail has been stepped on. I looked back and saw a girl spring up from her seat. Her name was Hua.

"You are most disloyal to Chairman Mao!" the girl screamed at Teacher Li. Anger made her round face red and the freckles near her nose more noticeable. Like most girls in my class, she had two braids dangling by her ears.

Teacher Li looked up, her eyebrows raised.

I was in disbelief. Disloyalty to Mao was a serious accusation. This was a time when being disloyal to Mao was equivalent to being counter-revolutionary and could lead to public humiliation, beating, imprisonment, or even death.

"You made our great leader Chairman Mao upside down!" Hua yelled at the teacher. The girl's head bobbed up and down, and her eyes were fixed on the teacher's face.

I was stunned by her accusation. It was very common to fold newspapers while reading them, and no one gave it a second thought. All 30 pairs of eyes were on Teacher Li. We held our breath. The room was so quiet that we could have heard a pin drop.

"This morning," Teacher Li said, "when military representative Uncle Lang was reading this article to us teachers, this was the way he was holding the newspaper. Are you saying the military representative was disrespectful to Chairman Mao? Sit down!" She pressed her left palm down in Hua's direction.

The girl still stood.

"Teacher Li," she said, "I saw some big-character posters that said you are a historical counter-revolutionary. Are you?"

It was like a drop of cold water falling in hot oil. Whispers rose from every corner of the quiet classroom. The students were stunned. Like me, they must not have read the big-character posters. Teacher Li looked as if she had been punched in the stomach. She stood there speechless, and her face changed colors a few times, from pale to red and back to pale again. I had never seen her like this. For the past three years that I had known her, she had always been composed. The students were quiet now, waiting for an answer.

Teacher Li walked from the side of the podium to the back and put down the newspaper. She then picked up Mao's quotation book from the top of the podium and started reading, "We should trust the masses. We should trust the party. These are the two fundamental principles. If we question these two principles, we will not be able to accomplish anything." This quotation gave me hope. I didn't want my teacher persecuted.

Teacher Li put the little red book on the podium and lifted her head to face her students. She opened her mouth as if she was going to say something, but she didn't. She took a deep breath and looked away at the window. I waited.

Finally, she looked at us and said, "I am not a historical counter-revolutionary." Her voice softened. "The revolutionary masses under the leadership of the military representatives will find that I am innocent." She managed to put on a smile, though it looked forced.

She picked up the newspaper and resumed reading the article. This time, she didn't fold it.

I didn't believe Teacher Li was a counter-revolutionary, especially a historical counter-revolutionary. A historical counter-revolutionary was someone who had been involved in activities against the Communist Party before 1949 when it took over China. Teacher Li was too young to be accused of that, I believed. As I looked at Teacher Li's awkward smile, my heart was heavy. *How awful must she have felt being accused of such a horrible crime?* I hoped it would turn out as Teacher Li had said and she would be exonerated.

The next morning, I went to school like it was any other day. The bell rang, but our teacher didn't show up. We waited. When we ran out of patience and started talking and giggling, a young female teacher popped her head in the door. "Why are you still sitting here?" she said. "Go downstairs. A revolution is being carried out."

We dashed out of the classroom and ran outside the building. Encircled by the U-shaped school building was a playground. A red brick stage sat at the end of the playground, against the building. It seemed that half of the school had already gathered here. Because the stage was on the west side of the building, we hadn't heard the crowd as we'd waited for Teacher Li in our east-facing classroom.

On the stage, a few older students were setting up a podium and testing loudspeakers. They were preparing for a mass rally. I couldn't understand why we hadn't been told about the rally ahead of time so that we could bring our little folding stools from home as we always did—and why was there no red banner stretched across the stage? All the rallies I had attended had had a red banner with the names of the targets on it. *Who is the rally against?* I wondered.

I zigzagged through the crowd to get closer to the stage. When I was about 10 feet away, I heard some commotion behind me. I looked back and saw a few male students half-dragging and half-carrying someone by the arms out of the building. The person was face down. The crowd parted, forming a path leading to the stage. When the students rushed by me, dragging the person with them, I recognized her from her familiar dark blue shirt and the shoulder-length black hair. I couldn't believe my eyes. Seeing my own teacher being dragged like a dead animal was the most terrible scene I had ever witnessed.

The students hauled Teacher Li up to the stage so quickly I suspected that her feet didn't even touch the steps. On the stage, she was forced to face the crowd and bend over. Two students grabbed her arms from behind and lifted them up as high as possible, and at the same time, they pushed her head down so low it looked as if she were examining her belly button. Through loudspeakers, some older students took turns denouncing her. They accused her of joining a youth group named the Three Principles of the People Youth League. The group was said to have been under the control of the Kuomintang government before the communists took over China. The fact that Teacher Li's parents were landlords didn't help her situation.

Between speeches, the crowd shouted slogans: "Eliminate the enemy if she doesn't surrender!" "Smash the dog head of Li!"

With each slogan, a student on the stage pulled Teacher Li's head up by her hair so that the "revolutionary mass" could see her "ugly counter-revolutionary face." Teacher Li's eyes were closed, and her face was ashen white against her dark blue shirt.

Someone among the students behind the teacher spat on her. A female student ordered the teacher not to clean up the stains left by the "little revolutionary fellows."

My heart was racing. I couldn't believe what was happening. Yesterday Teacher Li had been reading Mao's quotation and claiming her innocence. Today she was being abused by the students. Seeing my teacher suffer, I felt vulnerable and exposed. I had been seeking approval from Teacher Li ever since I had known her. Every faint smile or nod of her head was an encouragement to me. Now she was bending over, and a student on the stage was gripping her hair, pulling her head up and pushing it down every few minutes.

This is so scary. Please, someone, stop this, I pleaded under my breath. I looked around, hoping to see an adult. However, I was surrounded by only young faces; some were dazed, but many were excited.

There were no adults around, not even the woman who had told us about the rally. The military men were nowhere to be found even though they lived and worked at the school. At the time, it seemed that the rally was the students' spontaneous action. Only when I was older did I realize that the elementary school students couldn't have initiated and organized a rally against a teacher without the military men's permission and support. We had never had this kind of rally at our school before. The possibility cannot be ruled out that on that violent day, the military representatives orchestrated the whole thing and watched us from their office windows.

Around me was the frenzied crowd. I had seen the same craziness during all the other rallies. Agitation was in the air. There was a mixture of anxiety, anticipation, excitement, and even joy. People took pleasure in others' suffering. The ugly side of human nature stared at me once again.

As soon as I got home from the rally, I threw myself in bed and covered my face with a pillow. I felt like crying. I wanted to cry for Teacher Li and the horrific day, but I didn't. A little voice inside me said, *What if she is a class enemy? What if she did join the organization?*

At the dinner table, I told Mother that Teacher Li was in trouble.

Turning to me, Mother asked, "What kind of trouble?"

"We had a rally against her in school."

"A rally against a teacher?" Mother asked, stopping her chopsticks in the air.

"Our school had rallies against teachers, too," Big Brother said.

"Ours, too," Second Brother said.

"I know. You told me," Mother said to my brothers, "but your sister is in elementary school."

The dim ceiling light above the dining table cast a shadow on Mother's face; she looked worried.

That evening after dinner, I helped Mother clean up.

"Mom," I asked, wiping the table, "what is the Three Principles of the People Youth League?"

"Why do you ask?" Mother asked, stopping her sweeping of the concrete floor and looking directly at me. In her eyes, I saw concern, anxiousness, and even a little fear. I was surprised by her strong reaction.

"Is that a really bad organization?" I asked. I wanted to

know what kind of trouble Teacher Li was in. Mother didn't answer me.

"The students pulled Teacher Li's hair and spat on her during the rally because she joined the organization," I continued. Mother frowned, and she bit her lower lip as if she couldn't bear to hear what I had said.

"Just because the students said that Teacher Li joined the organization, doesn't mean she did," she said.

I felt somewhat relieved for Teacher Li.

"I don't want you to be disrespectful to Teacher Li," Mother added.

"I will not," I said, half-promising and half-protesting. I was surprised and even hurt that Mother felt the need to remind me of that. She should have known me better. I wouldn't disrespect my own teacher, although I couldn't honestly say I would never denounce some stranger standing before me in a meeting when I was asked to do so.

Mother finished sweeping the floor in a hurry and left the room.

There were too many things that I didn't understand. The articles in the newspapers described the Cultural Revolution as a dragnet catching every class enemy; now Teacher Li, the person who'd told me to support the Cultural Revolution, had been caught. I was lost.

I chose to blame the chaos and abuse on the students, not the government and the Purifying Class Ranks Movement. To continue my life in China, not only did I have to follow the party, but I also had to justify its policies when they brought horrifying consequences. It made it easier on my own conscience. *The party is great and flawless. It is the people, in this case, the students, who made mistakes,* I told myself. People's behaviors are learned. I had heard other people say things like this, so I said the same. I didn't think of questioning or criticizing the party because I had never heard anyone do that.

The next day at school, I saw Teacher Li in the hallway. She strode past me with her head lowered, still wearing the same dark blue shirt she'd worn the previous day. The stains from the students' spit had dried but were visible on her back.

Teacher Li was not allowed to teach anymore, though I did see her occasionally in school. She always walked quickly and never looked at anybody. I assumed she had been forced to write confessions somewhere in the building, as many people in a similar situation were forced to do at the time. I never thought of stopping her or asking her how she was doing, although I didn't believe she was a class enemy.

In Teacher Li's absence, other teachers took turns teaching us. But they had their own students to take care of. All they could do was get us started on a project before going back to teach their students.

Teacher Nie, a female teacher in her twenties, loved to make us write articles condemning everything that was not in line with the party's indoctrination, sometimes even ourselves. "I want you to write an article examining your own behaviors as a result of the bourgeois ideology influence," she would say. "I want you to write three pages by the end of the day. Write down all the selfish thoughts that you have had, even if they only lasted a split second." She would cast a slow, scrutinizing glance around the classroom as if her eyes were searchlights. She would add as she walked toward the door, "Don't you run around in the classroom. I will come back and check on you when you don't expect it." Then she would look back at us before closing the door behind her.

Teacher Gu was much more laid-back. Tall and baby-faced, he would lean on the radiators under the window of the classroom with his arms folded in front of his chest and his long legs stretched out. He made us draw hand grenades, guns, warships, or tanks in our notebooks.

Throughout the 10 years of the Cultural Revolution, Mao launched numerous shorter, overlapping political movements, each serving a particular purpose. While the nation was still engaging in the Purifying Class Ranks Movement, another movement, the City Youth Sent-Down Movement, started.

In the summer of 1968, two years after the government urged the youth from all over the nation to travel to Beijing to see Mao and to participate in the Cultural Revolution, it mobilized the youth again. This time, though, it sent the young people from cities to rural areas of China to do farmwork. By now, the military had hand-picked Mao's loyalists to form revolutionary committees to replace former leadership throughout the nation. When that was completed, the city youths' role of taking power from former officials and clearing the way for Mao's loyalists came to an end. By sending the young people from the cities to do forced labor in rural areas, where they were consumed by the daily struggle for survival, Mao removed the potential threat to the new power. "After the rabbit is killed, cook the hunting dogs" was a strategy often used by generations of Chinese rulers.

Unlike the frightening Purifying Class Ranks Movement, the Sent-Down Movement started like a giant celebration. Every day, I read or heard about mass send-off rallies where the sent-down youths were treated like heroes. Officials from the revolutionary committees pinned big red flowers made of paper or fabric on the city youths' chests and gave them Mao's books as gifts in farewell rallies. The government and the media told the people that the movement was the best thing for the nation as well as for the city youths. "It will narrow the gap between cities and the countryside, and the educated youths will make great achievements in the vast countryside," the media told the people. "We have two hands and will not dawdle in the cities," read a headline splashed in bold characters across the front page of the newspapers.

At the university, I saw hurried youths and their parents leaving campus, apparently on their way to the Beijing train station. The youths wore baggy unisex clothes that were similar to military uniforms in color and style. On their feet were the canvas shoes with rubber sides and bottoms that military men wore. It looked as if the parents were sending their youths to war.

In August, 18-year-old Big Brother received a sent-down notice. He was ordered to report to Northeastern China, an area next to Russia, to grow soybeans. The place was known as Big Northern Barren. He was to leave in a week.

Like other youths, Big Brother believed that he could do great good for the nation and himself by going to the countryside, even though it meant that his Hu Kou was about to be permanently transferred out of Beijing and to Big Northern Barren. The Hu Kou system, the Chinese household registration system, allowed the government to dictate where a person lived and worked. Once Big Brother's Hu Kou was transferred out, he would never be allowed to live or work in Beijing again unless he received special permission from the government. Big Brother appeared to be in high spirits as he packed and said goodbye to his friends who were being sent to other parts of the country.

The evening before he left Beijing, Big Brother played music in his room. I sat by him and listened. From the many instruments that he played, he chose Er Hu, a two-stringed bowed instrument that could produce a heartrending wail. He played and played. The beautiful, poignant music filled the room. An empty feeling came over me.

After Big Brother left, I sensed that something was not right at home. Although Mother still went to work as before, her infectious laughter gradually disappeared from our home. She and Second Brother often talked to each other in serious tones, but as soon as I walked into the room, the talk stopped.

"What are you talking about?" I would ask.

"You are too young to understand," Second Brother would say. Only 16 years old, he acted as if he were a grown-up.

One afternoon, two students, a male and a female from Mother's department, came to our home when Mother was at work. Since launching the Cultural Revolution two years earlier, the government had banned universities from accepting new students. The students who were already in the university stayed on to carry out the revolution full time.

"We are from your mother's study group," the woman said with a nasal voice. Her short, straight hair covered her ears and sandwiched her pointy face. The words "study group" gave me a chill.

To clean out people who were disloyal to him, not only did Mao launch the Purifying Class Ranks Movement, but he also provided the means. "The study group is a good method," Mao said in February 1968. A song was made based on Mao's quotation to praise the study group. When I first learned the song, I didn't know that the Mao Zedong Thought Study Groups were actually interrogation teams. By the time the two students from Mother's study group showed up, I already knew that the real goal of the group was to find counter-revolutionaries because I had schoolmates whose parents were being interrogated by the study groups.

In Mother's room, Second Brother and I sat side by side on the edge of the bed. The female student sat on a chair against the wall, facing us. The room was small, and my knees and hers almost touched. The male student positioned himself next to the female student, half-leaning and half-sitting on Mother's desk.

The woman told us the unthinkable: Mother was suspected of being a counter-revolutionary. All this time, when Mother went to work every day, she was being interrogated. I felt lightheaded, and I couldn't breathe. A counter-revolutionary was a bad person, heartless and against the people. Mother was nothing like that. I couldn't believe the person who was the closest to me in the world was facing the worst accusation imaginable.

I hung my head, feeling confused, panicked, and even ashamed.

"We want her to come back to Chairman Mao's proletarian revolutionary line," the male student said. He had a thick head of hair and a strong jawline. "All your mother needs to do is be honest with us. The party and the people will forgive her." He spoke quickly as if he had already run out of patience. "You need to help her understand it because it is about your future, also."

The man told us a story of a colleague of Mother's who was also under interrogation.

"You know Lan, your mother's colleague, don't you?" The man looked at Second Brother and me. I nodded, remembering the lanky middle-aged man who lived in the same area and always wore a dark blue cap.

"Lan refused our help at first, like your mother," the male student said, "but the study group didn't give up on him. Eventually, he recognized his dangerous situation. One night, he got up and kneeled in front of Chairman Mao's portrait, confessing all his counter-revolutionary thoughts. Now he will get lenient treatment."

The students stopped talking. They wanted to see our reaction. I knew they were expecting us to show our loyalty to Mao and our willingness to cooperate with Mother's interrogation group. In school, some of my friends had been forced to write open letters urging their parents to confess. The letters had been read through loudspeakers for everyone to hear. I remembered the words they'd used. I knew what to say in this situation, but I was counting on Second Brother to say something to satisfy the students because he was older.

But Second Brother was quiet. I looked at him. He wore a dark blue shirt with the long sleeves rolled up, a popular look at the time. He was thin, but his shoulders were wider than other 16-year-old boys'. Now his shoulders drooped, and his back hunched. That was his way of showing his disinterest.

The male student adjusted his position on the desk. He seemed to be getting impatient. The silence in the room became unbearable. I was getting nervous. The window was open, but the air felt heavy. *I must say something*, I thought. As I was contemplating what to say, Second Brother burst into laughter. Puzzled, the students stared at him. I was worried for Second Brother. Laughing at the wrong time or in front of the wrong people could bring trouble. *Is he laughing at Lan because he knelt in front of Mao's portrait?* I wondered. It was not wise to laugh at someone for demonstrating his loyalty to Mao, especially in the presence of the interrogation group.

Second Brother sat up straight, and his head tilted back when he laughed. When he finally finished laughing, he wiped his eyes with his palm. After that, he slumped and fell silent.

The students looked at each other. It seemed they didn't know what to do. Before they took off, the female student recited to us a line that we had heard every day: "You can't choose which family you were born into, but you can choose which path you take." In their eyes, we had been born into a bad family. Being children of educated parents was a birth defect in Mao's China and a cause for discrimination.

I closed the door after the students were gone and ran back to Mother's room.

"You can't choose which family you were born into." Second Brother pinched his nose with his fingers to sound nasal, mocking the woman. Unlike me, who wanted to believe everything I was told and to please everyone, Second Brother was rebellious.

"Why did you laugh that hard? What was so funny?" I asked, thankful that he had made the students go away.

"I wanted them to know that I wasn't afraid," he said, puffing out his chest.

"Don't tell Mom the students were here," he said. He sounded like an adult. I nodded.

But Mother knew. The students told her that they had been at our home to "work on us."

After dinner, Mother explained her "situation" to me.

Second Brother had gone back to his room. He had known what was happening to Mother at work all along. Mother looked me squarely in the eye and said slowly, "Listen: I don't have serious issues. I want you to remember that."

During the Cultural Revolution, the people who were being interrogated as counter-revolutionaries were said to "have issues."

I nodded. Mother sat back in her chair and told me that when she entered middle school in 1938, 11 years before the communists took over China, she joined the Three Principles of the People Youth League. My heart sank. It was the same organization that Teacher Li had joined.

"I was only 13 at the time," Mother said. "And our whole class joined it together. Everyone had to." She told me not to worry. "I have told the organization about my past in every political movement. I am not hiding anything." Chinese people called the Communist Party "the organization." Mother reassured me that she was cooperating with the interrogation group and her case would be closed soon.

I said nothing. I shivered when I thought about the chaotic scene at the rally against Teacher Li.

I didn't tell Mother that I was afraid for her because she had enough to worry about already. The Cultural Revolution had taught me to keep worries and fears to myself. There was no use telling anyone. No one could stop the bad things from happening, not the professors who were forced to kneel in front of our window and not Teacher Li, whose hair had been pulled by the students.

In the giant meat grinder known as Mao's China, individuals were powerless. Parents could not protect their children. They couldn't even defend themselves.

CHAPTER FOUR

1969

In late spring, the government sent Second Brother to Yunnan province, an area adjacent to Vietnam, to grow rice and be re-educated by the peasants.

The evening before Second Brother left, I watched him pack. The upper level of the bunk bed in his room used to be Big Brother's. Now a violin, an Er Hu, and some other musical instruments were laid side by side on the bed. Big Brother had wanted to bring his violin with him, but Mother had talked him out of the idea. Although youths received hero-like treatment in the send-off ceremonies, Mother knew that being sent down was a punishment. Children of educated parents were labeled "could-be-reformed children," implying they could not be trusted until they were reformed. Bringing a violin would have been like drawing a big bull's-eye on Big Brother's forehead, showing the peasants that he was not willing to give up his bourgeois way of living.

I sat down on the lower bed. Facing me against the wall was a table. A small chalkboard hung on the wall next to the table.

Second Brother put a large sheet of blue plastic on the floor and spread a quilt over it. He then put his clothes in the middle of the quilt and folded it into a flat, square bundle with the clothes in it. Afterward, he used a rope to tie up the bundle, making a three-by-three grid as in a tic-tac-toe game. He then made two loops with a rope and tied them to the bundle so that he could carry it on his back to the train.

"When are you coming back?" I asked. I had the same empty feeling that I'd had the night before Big Brother left.

"Soon," he said.

"How soon?"

"I will be back for the next Chinese New Year."

I counted in my head. It would be 10 months before I could see him again. I sighed.

After dragging the baggage to the corner of the room, he drew a little house on the chalkboard. He then added a bird on the roof. I watched him and felt a lump in my throat. It felt as if it had been just yesterday that my brothers were still boys, making wood handguns or sneaking into the military's shooting range to find shell casings. Now Second Brother was leaving home to work the fields. He was just 16. Not only did I worry about Second Brother, but I also worried about Mother. *Who will talk to her after a day of interrogation? And what if the students come back?* I thought. My eyes were burning. I tried hard not to cry.

When I woke up the next morning, Second Brother was gone.

Every day, I walked into my brothers' room and looked at the empty bunk bed and the bird that Second Brother had drawn, and I counted the days to the Chinese New Year. About a week after Second Brother left, I was shocked to see the chalkboard had been cleaned. Mother had done it. I couldn't believe it. Seeing the bird Second Brother had drawn had been like hearing his promise to come home, but now the bird was gone. I picked up a piece of chalk and traced the faint lines that were still visible on the chalkboard, but the head of the bird was completely erased. The eye, the beak, and the feathers on top of the head were all gone. I started crying.

Mother apologized, but I continued crying. I had been looking for an excuse to cry since Second Brother had left home. There were too many things worth crying about these days: Teacher Li's persecution, my brothers' being sent away, and Mother's interrogation. I tried to believe the government, which told us that "the situation in the nation is extraordinarily great and is getting even greater" while my world was falling apart.

The same two students who had come to our home before came again when Mother was at work.

In Mother's room, the students went through the dresser and every drawer in the desk. Books, notebooks, pens, and papers quickly piled up on Mother's desk. The male student even opened the letters. I stood in the middle of the room, watching and wondering if they would have done so if Second Brother had been at home.

Not finding anything interesting in the letters, the male student turned to me and asked me if my mother had burned anything lately. He had a regional accent. In Chinese, the word "burn" (Shao) sounds the same as the word "send" or "deliver" in some regional dialects. I thought he was asking me if Mother had sent anything out.

"No," I said. "But she is about to."

"What is she going to burn? Show me." The male slammed a drawer and rushed over. Excited, he puffed up like a blowfish, chest out and arms stuck out from the sides of his body.

I led the two students into my brothers' room, where a package sat on the table by the wall.

"We will send this package to my second brother this weekend," I said.

Second Brother and his fellow sent-down youths didn't have enough to eat. A few months after he had left Beijing,

Mother and I received a photo from him. For his 17th birthday, Second Brother had gone to a nearby town and had his picture taken in a studio. We had been shocked by his appearance. He had changed: he was dark, and his eyes were deeply set and big. His cheekbones stuck out. He'd lost so much weight that his shirt was dangling from his shoulders like it was on a clothes hanger.

"What has happened to him?" Mother had asked, holding the photo with both hands and studying it carefully. "This is more than just the result of hard work."

From Second Brother's short but frequent letters, we'd learned that he was having a tough time in the countryside. Although breathtakingly beautiful, with palm trees and lush green landscapes, Yunnan had a punishing climate for farmworkers. In the hot and humid climate, rice matured two or three times a year instead of once a year as in colder areas, which meant farmworkers worked hard all year long. The villagers didn't have tractors or other machinery and were not even accustomed to using shovels. Instead, they still used primitive tools like knives and fire to farm. Before planting, they found a piece of barren land and set it on fire to kill everything: weeds, bugs, and so on. Then, instead of plowing the land, they dug holes with long knives in the soil before putting seeds in them, one hole at a time, under the tropical sun. The next year, they would abandon the land, find another piece of barren land, set it on fire, and start all over again.

Second Brother's photo had worried Mother. She'd immediately written a letter to him demanding an answer.

It turned out that even more challenging than performing backbreaking labor was hunger. There was simply not enough food.

Less than 10 years after the peasants received farmland as the result of the Land Reform Movement, the land was taken away by the government and put in the government-controlled people's communes. Peasants became slaves. They worked on the land that they didn't own, and they were not allowed to live anywhere else. Under the government's orders, Second Brother's village grew rice and rice only. Even the rice that was harvested was to be sent to the government to satisfy the quota first.

During the Great Leap Forward Movement between 1958 and 1962, peasants were forced to submit more crops than they harvested. The result was that tens of millions of peasants starved to death in three years. To end the catastrophe, against Mao's will, then-Chairman Liu Shaoqi and other like-minded leaders of China implemented new policies in 1962 allowing peasants to grow a small quantity of vegetables and herbs on the small plots of land around their residences. Peasants were also allowed to raise chickens, pigs, and so on. The new policies saved millions of lives. During the Cultural Revolution, however, these lifesaving measures became evidence proving that Liu Shaoqi was a capitalist-roader and should be purged, though the peasants in many areas were still allowed to grow small quantities of food and raise small animals for their own consumption.

During the Sent-Down Movement, Second Brother and other sent-down youths worked side by side with the peasants. However, the city youths were not allowed to raise animals or grow their own vegetables.

The sent-down youths protested, "But all villagers raise animals!"

"Peasants don't need to be re-educated," the village head said. "The 'could-be-reformed children' need to learn to endure hardship."

So, the youths from the cities did hard labor but ate no eggs and no meat. Rice and vegetables digested fast, and the youths constantly battled hunger.

"This is so unfair," I'd said to Mother after reading Second Brother's letter. I didn't understand why he and other sent-down youths had gotten on the train as "revolutionary youths" and gotten off the train as "could-be-reformed children."

Since then, Mother had been periodically sending food to Second Brother to compensate for the food shortage: dried shredded pork, dried fruits, and candies. When the two students came, we had just prepared another food package for Second Brother.

"Did your mother burn anything with fire?" the male student asked me again, realizing that I'd misunderstood him.

"No." I shook my head.

Without saying a word, he walked back to Mother's room and made loud noises, opening and closing drawers.

The woman and I stayed in my brothers' room.

"How old are you?" the woman asked. Her voice was much softer than the man's.

"Eleven," I answered.

"You can write many Chinese characters, then?"

I nodded.

"Your mother is in a lot of trouble," she said. "She refuses the revolutionary masses' help." She pointed at the chalkboard. "I want you to write something to help your mother." I picked up a piece of chalk and waited.

"Write: 'Confess, and you will be treated leniently; resist, and you will be punished severely,'" the woman said with a smile.

This slogan was seen everywhere: on the walls, on the banners, in the newspapers, or on the stages of the mass rallies.

I followed her order, although I felt uncomfortable writing such a hostile phrase on the blackboard.

"Oh, look, you know all the characters. How wonderful," the woman cheered.

"Don't erase it," she said. "Let your mother see it. You want to help your mother, don't you?"

The two took off.

As much as I loved Mother, and as much as I knew the phrase on the blackboard would hurt her, I kept it there.

Looking back decades later, I still can't explain why. At the time, it never occurred to me that I didn't have to follow the order. There was no real danger for me if I erased the slogan.

In late fall, Father came home. It was a surprise visit.

That morning, I walked out of our apartment, turned left, and saw Father walking up the stairs. He had a blue hat on and two duffle bags on his shoulder, one in the front and one in the back. I couldn't believe my eyes. I hadn't known he was coming back. No one in our family had. Usually, he would send a telegram notifying us of his trip, but not this time.

My heart almost jumped out of my chest. "Baba!" I called out. Baba was Chinese for "dad." Father smiled, standing in front of me. Surprised, I didn't know what to do except beam from ear to ear.

With Father home, Mother became a different person. The woman who had been under tremendous pressure now wore a constant smile. During Father's vacation, my parents often called each other by the nicknames they'd used when they'd first met. They would look at each other, smiling, without saying a word. Sometimes, when he was reading by the desk, Mother would point at him, motioning to me to sneak up on him and tickle him. When he protested, she would laugh.

Seeing my parents together gave me a great sense of security. Life was normal again.

The poplar trees that lined the streets of Beijing turned golden. In the wind, their heart-shaped leaves swirled off the branches and piled up on the ground. There they dried and turned brown, crunching and crumbling under people's feet. Winter was coming. After spending about a month with us, it was almost time for Father to go back to Qinghai. Mother rushed to finish off a sweater that she had been knitting for him.

On one bright and crisp afternoon near the end of Father's vacation, Father, Mother, and I went to the Summer Palace. In the heart of the centuries-old imperial garden, Kunming Lake glistened under the blue sky. A forested shoreline to the west bordered the lake like an elegant wreath. To the north, pavilions nestled into the evergreen trees on the hillside. To the south, a long stone bridge extended into the middle of the lake and reached a lone island.

It was cold, and people were in their winter jackets. As always, we rented a rowboat. Father and I took turns rowing the little wooden boat while Mother sat in the back. To avoid the loudspeakers on the bank, we rowed the boat to the 17-Arch Bridge in the middle of Kunming Lake. The arched white marble bridge connected the east bank and an island in the center of the lake like a beautiful rainbow. As always, I wanted to row the boat through the center arch of the bridge. And as always, I lost my nerve when I got closer to the bridge because some other boats were trying to do the same thing. I hesitated, fearing that I would hit other boats or the bridge.

"I will go through the arch next to the middle one," I said and started to turn the boat.

"Don't be afraid," Father said with a smile. "If you set out to go through the biggest arch, then you should do it. I will help you." He had a blue cotton-padded jacket on but no hat. Behind him in the distance was Longevity Hill, covered with evergreen trees. On top of the hill stood the Tower of Buddhist Incense, decorated with golden tiles and red paint.

I straightened out the boat and aimed at the center arch. It was at least 20 feet wide and 30 feet deep, with a few boats congregated underneath. Near-collisions happened a few times as we made our way through. Each time, Father gave the other rowboat a gentle push, avoiding a crash.

After I had passed the center arch, Father took over the boat. He rowed it around the island and then toward the west. By the time we reached the west bank, the sun was about to drop behind the Western Hills, and the ripples around us were painted golden by the setting sun. Father stopped rowing, letting the boat drift on the water.

"Go sit with your dad," Mother said to me. "I will take a picture of the two of you." I moved over and sat down next to Father. "Smile," she said and took the last photo of the day before it became completely dark.

It was the last photo I had with Father.

Afterward, we sat quietly in the little rowboat as the darkness swallowed us. We hadn't noticed before, but the loudspeakers had stopped. The park was so quiet now that we could hear the water gently rushing against the Jade Belt Bridge 20 feet away. For a long time, no one said anything. We listened to the sound of the water, looked at the purple mountains in the distance, and enjoyed being with each other. Time seemed to have stopped. Looking back, I wish time had frozen forever at that moment.

"This time, when I go back to Qinghai," Father said, "I will go to a cadre school in Henan province."

This was news to me, and Mother also seemed surprised. She looked at Father as if she was trying to figure out what the news meant.

Since 1968, many so-called cadre schools had been set up in China. Almost every university and government entity had one. They were farms created for former officials and educated people to do hard manual labor and reform their worldview. Father must have had no choice; otherwise, he would have discussed it with Mother instead of casually mentioning it in the middle of Kunming Lake. He made it sound as if going to the cadre school was his decision. Years later, we would find out that he had been put on the list by the military men and the list was not really for the cadre school.

"Good," Mother said. She lifted her chin as she always did when she made up her mind. "I will join you there. Our daughter can come with me. I am sure there are schools for children there. Maybe our sons can be transferred there, too. They are doing physical labor anyway. That way, we will be together."

Father didn't say anything. He looked at Mother and then looked away.

In the distance, the rolling Western Hills wore different shades of purple, looking mysterious against the darkening sky. The lights that lined the bank of the lake had come on, and the smooth water reflected the light like a mirror. Once in a while, a rowboat passed by, breaking the mirror into many little trembling pieces.

"Qinghai Lake is always pitch-black because the water is deep, not like the water in Kunming Lake, always so clear," Father said. His voice was so calm that it sounded as if he was talking to himself. From his voice, I could tell how much he missed his hometown and his family. After spending nine years away, he must have been tired in body and soul. I looked down into the water. The water in Kunming Lake was pitch-black at this time of the day. I scooped up water with my hands. It was bone-chillingly cold.

When snow covered the ancient city like a blanket, Father left.

He never returned.

❧

The usual dinnertime had long passed, and Mother hadn't come home. I was frantic.

I looked out the window. It was dark. A lone streetlight was dangling from the top of a light pole, giving out a dim yellowish glow. Swinging back and forth in the wind, the metal lampshade made a distinct sound each time it hit the light pole. The giant shadow of the apartment building shifted on the ground with each swing of the light. The streets were empty.

I decided to go to Mother's office inside the academic area to look for her. The campus was divided into two regions: a residential area and an academic area. The residential area had apartments, stores, cafeterias, swimming pools, gyms, and so on. The academic area was a restricted area with office buildings, classrooms, and libraries hidden inside the walls and behind the wrought iron gate, which was guarded by a civilian guard. Unless escorted by university employees, children were not allowed inside the academic area. I planned to beg the guard to let me in.

I put on a dark-brown hooded jacket and stepped out of the building. It was even windier than I had thought. At the corner of the building, a gust of wind pushed me back. I took a big gulp of cold air and gathered myself. I bent down and headed into the wind.

When I arrived at the academic area, I realized that the situation was worse than I'd feared: the gate was locked. The reception office, where the guard stayed during the daytime, was inside the gate. The door to the office was closed, and the light was not on. I repeatedly shouted, "Anybody inside?" No one answered. The wind swallowed my words.

I looked inside the gate. The paved street sandwiched between office buildings was empty. Without lights, the buildings looked like mysterious giants, dark and silent.

From the gate, I couldn't see the chemistry department building, but I knew that at least one room still had a light on and Mother was in that room either being interrogated or being forced to write confessions. I was only a few hundred yards away from her. If I could hop over the gate, I would be able to find her, but the gate was taller than an adult. The tips of the vertical metal bars on the gate were sharp. I didn't think I could climb it. The gaps between the metal bars were too small for me to squeeze through.

It was so late that even the loudspeakers on top of the buildings were silent. The only sound was the wind howling in my ears. Standing under the yellowish glow of the streetlight, I had never felt so alone and so desperate. I wished Father or my brothers were with me. I squatted down and started crying.

Outside the gate and on my right-hand side was a small grove of pine trees. The wind wrestled through the trees, making a low roar like a caged animal. I got scared and stood up. It seemed in every dark shadow there could be someone hidden: in the corners of the buildings, under the low hedges along the street, or behind the bulletin board, where big-character posters were pasted and faded.

I turned around and started running home. The plastic soles of my shoes made a loud noise on the hard surface of the road. Hot from running, I took off the hood and unbuttoned my jacket. When I got closer to our apartment building, I saw a light coming from our window.

A cheerful voice rose inside me: *Mom is home.* I counted the windows again. Yes. It was Mother's room. She had told me when I was little: "Count from the right. The eighth window is ours. When you see the light is on, you know I am home."

A warm feeling spread through my body. I raced to the building, ran upstairs, and dashed into our apartment, but Mother's room was empty. I went to my room, which had been my brothers' room before they were sent down. She wasn't there, either. I checked the kitchen and the bathroom. No one was there. Mother wasn't home. I must have left the light on when I'd gone out. I stood in Mother's room, not knowing what to do. Disappointed and afraid, I wanted to cry, but I didn't. Instead, I gathered myself and did the only thing that I could think of: I walked to our neighbor's door.

Two years after the Cultural Revolution started, to lessen the housing shortage, almost half of the households in our apartment building had been required to accept another family to share the apartment with. We'd emptied one of the three rooms in our apartment for a family: a young female math teacher, her seven-month-old son, and the son's grandmother. The young woman's husband, a worker whose last name was Gao, worked outside Beijing, and we did not see him until half a year later. Though they were not our relatives, the two families got along, and I called them by familial names: Aunt Gao and Grandma Gao.

During the most difficult time of Mother's life, when some of her friends and colleagues shunned her to "draw a clear line" between themselves and a potential counter-revolutionary, she received solace and support from the Gao family, especially Grandma Gao, a petite woman with gray hair.

To divide and conquer, the communist government gave

everyone a "class status" based on their occupations in pre-communist China. When the communists took over China, Grandma Gao was in her forties and had a tailoring business that her late husband had left behind. The communist government labeled her a "small handicraft person," which didn't belong to either the exploiting class or the exploited class. Because of that, Grandma Gao was not a target of the revolution, and at the same time, she was not fond of it because she couldn't have a business anymore since the communists didn't allow it. Unemployed, she had no superiors to report to and no one watched over her, either. Only semi-literate, she ignored most of the propaganda in the newspapers. Most unemployed people in our residential area were made to attend political studies regularly, but Grandma Gao didn't. It might have been because she had a young grandson to take care of or because her son-in-law was a worker, a proletarian who was automatically considered a revolutionary. For whatever reason, Grandma Gao stayed under the radar. The unique situation allowed her to escape conformity and group thinking. The mind that was not contaminated by the "noble" ideology allowed logic and common sense. In the nationwide symphony praising Mao and the Communist Party during the Cultural Revolution, Grandma Gao played a different tune.

With Father and my brothers away, Grandma Gao became the person in whom Mother confided. Often, when Mother came home after exhausting and agonizing interrogations, Grandma Gao would pull her from the hallway into the Gaos' room. They would talk behind the closed door for a long time. I couldn't hear their conversations, but more than once, I heard Mother say to Grandma Gao on her way out, "I don't know what silly thing I would have done if it wasn't for you." Mother didn't know that at age 11, I was old enough to understand that the "silly thing" she referred to was committing suicide. It was a time when some people killed themselves to escape persecution. Hearing Mother mention the "silly thing" scared me. I was thankful to Grandma Gao for being there for Mother.

On this windy night, when Mother didn't come home, I knocked on the Gaos' door. Grandma Gao came out of the room and closed the door behind her.

"Little Red Moon has just fallen asleep," she whispered. Little Red Moon was her grandson's name. "Your Aunt Gao isn't home. The boy acted up and didn't want to go to sleep." Grandma Gao had a gray cotton-padded jacket on. Though it was late, the mandarin collar of her jacket was still buttoned up neatly. Her gray hair, which was made into a hair bun behind her head, didn't look as tidy as during the daytime. She looked a little tired.

"What's the matter?" she asked me. "Why are you wearing a winter jacket?"

"Mother hasn't come home yet," I said, holding back tears.

"Did your mother say anything before she left this morning?"

"Nothing unusual, but she left me a note."

We walked into Mother's room.

"Where is it?" Grandma Gao asked, looking around.

I picked up a piece of paper from Mother's desk and showed her.

"Read it," Grandma Gao said. "What does it say? I don't have my reading glasses with me." She looked nervous. Her eyes were fixed on my face. The wrinkles at the corners of her mouth deepened.

"It tells me to buy steamed buns from the cafeteria after school," I said.

Grandma Gao thought for a second. "How many did she want you to buy?"

"Five," I answered, puzzled by her question.

"How many do you usually buy?"

"Five. They will last two days."

"Oh. I think your mother is fine," she said. Years later, when I thought about that night, I realized Grandma Gao was afraid that Mother had committed suicide. "She is being kept by the people in her study group, like one of the women in your Aunt Gao's office," Grandma Gao said. "Go to bed. Your mother will be home. If she doesn't come home tonight, I will tell your Aunt Gao to look for her in the morning. Your Aunt Gao is not home now." Grandma Gao rubbed her face. "People are possessed nowadays."

To make their targets confess, the interrogation groups were often in session day and night, questioning the targets and exerting pressure on them. When one interrogator was tired, another would take over. The tactic was called the "spinning wheel." Exhausted and scared, many people under interrogation would make up stories to avoid even more severe punishments. I assumed Mother was under spinning wheel interrogation.

There was nothing Grandma Gao and I could do for Mother that night. I couldn't file a missing person report because the police were nonexistent at the time and all power belonged to the military people who had ordered Mother's interrogations.

I sank into Mother's big green bamboo armchair after Grandma Gao had left. The room had never seemed so quiet and so empty. I was worried about Mother. *Has she eaten? Is she being interrogated now, or is she sleeping? When is she coming home?* I thought about Father and my brothers, wondering what they would do if they were in my situation.

I was tired, but I didn't want to go back to my room. I was afraid that Mother would come home in the middle of the night and I wouldn't know. I climbed into Mother's bed and lay down. From the pillow, I detected a faint, familiar scent. It was the lotion that Mother used. I buried my face in the pillow and started to cry.

On the wall facing the bed was Mao's portrait. Mao had been watching us for more than three years. He'd watched our family suffer through the Cultural Revolution like many other families in the country. He'd watched as the Red Guards had raided our home several times; he'd watched as the armed revolutionaries had forced another family into our apartment; he'd watched as my brothers had terminated their education and been sent far away to do farmwork; and now he watched me cry because I didn't know what had happened to Mother. Later, he would watch our family suffer the loss of Father. He watched it all with that frozen smile on his face.

As dawn broke the next morning, two students arrived. I recognized the young man and woman as the two people who had raided our apartment not long before.

"Your mother is stubborn and resists our help," the male student with a square face said to me. He stuck his hand into his thick, disheveled hair and scratched his head hard. "You are coming with us," he said. "You need to convince your mother to confess."

"Where is my mother?" I asked.

"We have her. Come with us."

"It is time for your mother to think about your future, not just herself," the female student said. "We trust that you will help her make the right choice."

I followed the students out of our apartment.

As we passed the Gaos' room, the door was open, and Grandma Gao was holding up the blue curtain in the doorway and waiting for us. Although it was early, she seemed to have been up for a while. Her gray hair was neat and smooth. Her eyes shifted between the students and me. Somehow I felt she looked like an alert, elegant bird. She motioned for me to come into her room.

The male student put his hand on the door frame to stop me from going in. "What are you trying to do?" he said to Grandma Gao. "Don't you interfere with our work." Frustration was written on his face.

Grandma Gao smiled. "Young fellow, have a little patience." Having a worker son-in-law, Grandma Gao was considered to be on the revolutionary side and was less fearful than most people. I suspected she got to keep her hair bun for the same reason. Most women's hair buns, including Father's mother's, had been cut off by Mao's loyalists at the beginning of the Cultural Revolution because they were thought to be a symbol of the old culture.

Grandma Gao pointed at me. "The child didn't have breakfast yet," she said to the male student. "I will give her a quick bite, and then she will go with you."

The student took his hand off the door frame. I went into the Gaos' room while the students waited in the hallway. Grandma Gao let down the curtain.

The room was small. A big bed and a few pieces of simple furniture occupied most of the room, leaving only an area of about two feet by seven feet of concrete floor uncovered. As a result, almost all activities were done in bed. The small desk jammed between a wall and the bed served multiple purposes. Now it was a breakfast table with a few steamed buns and a small plate of pickled vegetables on it.

Grandma Gao lowered her voice. "I hope they will let your mother come home tonight, but I don't know what will happen." She picked up a steamed bun from the table, put it in my hand, and continued whispering into my ear. "You need to be smart. When you get there, look around. Remember where your mother is, which room she is locked up in, and who is there watching her." She kept looking at the blue curtain that separated the students from the room. "This way," she said, "if she doesn't come home, we will know where to find her."

I nodded. I didn't eat the steamed bun. I was too upset.

Grandma Gao wrapped the bun in a white handkerchief and put it in the pocket of my winter jacket. "Give it to your mother," she said.

I followed the two students to the chemistry department building and was led to a room on the third floor. It was a big room with fluorescent lights hanging from the ceiling. Sitting on a chair in the middle of the room, facing the door, was Mother. In front of her were three yellow desks that were shoved together lengthwise to make one long table. Three people, two students and a middle-aged woman who was a teacher living in our residential area, were on the opposite side of the desks from Mother. They and the other two students who had come to fetch me formed an interrogation group.

The room went quiet when I walked in. I noticed that just as in the rally against Teacher Li, there were no military people present. It was a common tactic during the Cultural Revolution. The organizers stayed behind the scenes while the revolutionary masses carried out their orders. When excessive cruelty occurred that caused severe bodily harm or even death, the crimes could be blamed on the masses, which meant no one would be held responsible.

I sat in a chair on the students' side, facing Mother.

Mother seemed to be surprised to see me. She looked at me and looked away. I had a feeling that she didn't want me to be here. She looked tired, but her shoulder-length hair was neat, and her gray cardigan was clean. There were no signs of physical abuse. I felt somewhat relieved.

"There is still somebody's name that you are hiding from

us," the square-faced male student said to Mother.

I was surprised. All this time that Mother had been under investigation, I'd thought all she needed to do was criticize herself for joining a wrong group and being born into a landlord family and, therefore, having bourgeois thoughts. Her parents had owned 10 acres of farmland in pre-communist China, which qualified them as class enemies. Grandfather spent 10 years in a reform-through-labor camp because of it. This was the first time I realized that the interrogation group wanted Mother to give up someone's name.

I was nervous because I had heard that people who couldn't or wouldn't give the revolutionaries the information they wanted had suffered horrific consequences. I had been told that in the second year of the Cultural Revolution, the chancellor of the university had been beaten to death by two students because he'd refused to admit that he owned handguns. They'd beaten him so savagely that it was said his battered body looked as if he had a pair of red shorts on.

"I already told you everything I know," Mother said, looking at the table in front of her. She spoke with a clear voice, making sure every word was heard.

"You need to recognize the situation that you are in. Resisting does you no good!" The male student was loud and rude, practically barking. It saddened me to see Mother being treated like a criminal.

All of a sudden, the student turned to me. "Why don't you talk to your mother?"

Now all eyes were on me. I was nervous. *What should*

I say? I wanted to ask if Mother had slept last night. I wanted to tell her that I missed her and I was scared. But I didn't because that was not what was expected of me. I remembered the words that my friends used in their open letters, urging their parents to confess. I knew that was what the interrogation group wanted me to say, but I was reluctant to say it because it would hurt Mother.

I remembered the steamed bun that Grandma Gao had given to me. I reached into my pocket and took it out. It was still warm. I got up and walked to the tables between Mother and me. I wanted to give it to her. The middle-aged woman stood up and took the steamed bun. Wrapped inside her oversized military-green winter jacket, she looked sick, and her face was an unhealthy shade of yellowish-brown.

"What your mother needs now is not food but your help," the woman said to me in a stern voice. I looked at her and caught a cold glare.

"Your mother ate," the woman said. She turned to Mother. "Didn't we give you a steamed bun?"

"Yes. You did," Mother answered.

"Didn't we even warm it up for you on the radiator?" the woman asked again.

"Yes. You did. I was very moved by that."

Turning to me, the woman said, "See, we are not abusing your mother. We execute the party's policies precisely. We are helping her. Now it's your turn to help her." Looking down at me, the woman lacked facial expression. Her cheekbones stuck out from her fleshless face. She put the steamed bun back in my hand.

The room was quiet. Everyone was waiting. I had to say something. My mouth was dry. I wished my brothers were in the room. If they were, I wouldn't have to say anything because they were older. *And Father, if only he were here.*

I knew Mother was not a counter-revolutionary. Twenty years earlier, like many young and impressionable college students of her time, Mother had joined many protests organized by underground communists against the Kuomintang government, though she was not a Communist Party member. "I was a progressive youth who was frustrated by the corrupt government," Mother had told me.

In the late 1940s, China had just survived eight years of war against the Japanese and was in a civil war between the Kuomintang government and the communists. To a student like Mother, who was facing unemployment upon graduation in a country with galloping inflation, the communists' promise to build an American-style democratic government had tremendous appeal; sadly, it had proven to be a lie, which had become apparent soon after they'd taken power.

If I had been in a normal society under normal circumstances, I would have turned to the students and told them that I knew Mother was not a counter-revolutionary. If I had been a brave child, I would have told them they were wrong for keeping Mother. But I wasn't, and I had never heard anyone talk like that. In a nation where everyone was forced to conform, we all sounded alike. We said what was expected. Although I knew Mother was not hiding anything, I still had to say what Mother's interrogation group wanted me to say. It was just the way it was. Molded and shaped in a dictatorship, we could only repeat the party's doctrine instead of forming and expressing thoughts of our own. Not only did the dictator and his followers control our actions, but they also controlled our thoughts and emotions. We didn't ask ourselves how we really felt because how we felt didn't matter. We were trained to figure out what was expected of us at a young age.

"Why don't you just tell the truth, and it will be good for you and good for us," I said to Mother.

What I said didn't surprise anyone. It was an act. It was like a line an actor had to deliver. The Cultural Revolution was a giant stage, and everyone had to perform on it. What surprised me was the cold and distant tone in my voice. Not only had I obeyed the orders as I always did, but I had also chosen to side with the aggressors, not Mother, whom I knew was innocent. If I was acting, I played the role well.

Mother looked at me as I was talking. I thought I caught a hint of disapproval in her glance, but I wasn't sure. *Is she disappointed in me? Was she surprised by my tone?* I had no courage to say anything different, and I didn't even have the courage not to say anything.

Not being supportive of Mother when she needed me the most is the one thing I did during the Cultural Revolution of which I am most ashamed. When the Cultural Revolution was over, I told Mother I felt bad for not supporting her that day. She brushed it off by saying, "You were young. You were scared." I hoped Mother was right. I hoped my lack of courage was due to my young age. I didn't want to think that thousands of years of ruthless control by dictators had bred the last ounce of courage out of us.

When I reflected on the Cultural Revolution, I realized that the reason the nightmare lasted so long and became so atrocious was not only because of Mao or his loyalists, who knew their roles as the party's attack dogs. One important reason the Cultural Revolution became such a long-drawn-out calamity, through which so many people suffered, was that the majority of the people, people like me, who still had a conscience and who could still tell right from wrong, complied due to a lack of courage and fear of being on the wrong side. Compliance and conformity, either to a dictator's rules or a dominating opinion, was the easiest thing to do. However, it was also the most dangerous. No one is safe under a dictatorship. Bystanders in silence only postpone their own suffering or even death. During the Cultural Revolution, when people were being victimized, bystanders watched in silence. The result was hundreds of thousands, if not millions, of deaths.

The square-faced student, whom I believed to be the head of the interrogation group, said to Mother, "The military representatives in the department want to close your case before the Chinese New Year. It has been long enough. People have demonstrated plenty of mercy for you." He handed Mother a piece of paper and continued: "Today is your last chance. It is time for you to choose either resisting our help to the end or telling us what you know. Look at the names you have given to us so far and tell us the name that you are hiding. Now your fate and your children's future are in your hands."

Mother bowed her head and looked at the paper for a long time. Everyone was waiting. The room was so quiet that I could hear the buzzing sound of the fluorescent lights above my head. Increasingly impatient, the male student started cracking his knuckles one by one, making a loud noise in the otherwise quiet room.

"I have given you every name I can think of," Mother said. She lifted her head and put the piece of paper on the table in front of her.

The male student hit the table with his hand so hard that it startled me. "Hu Liang," he called out.

"Oh. Yes. I knew him," Mother said. She lowered her head.

The room was silent for a long time.

"You can go now," the middle-aged woman said to me.

I walked out of the room, feeling numb. I couldn't process what had just happened. The only thing I could think of was the loud sound made by the student's fist when he'd hit the table and the name he'd screamed out. I had never heard that name before. It was cold; I put my hands in my pockets. The steamed bun was still there. It was cold now.

Late that night, Mother came home.

She told me that after a few months of the investigation, the interrogation group had been ready to close her case when two men had come from the area where she'd gone to middle school. The men from Hubei province had wanted Mother to confirm someone's activities. However, they wouldn't tell her the name of that person. They'd asked her to tell them everyone she'd known in Hubei. When she couldn't give the name they wanted, they'd accused her of covering for the person. To help the men from Hubei province, Mother's study group at the department had interrogated her every day.

Mother explained to me that Hu Liang had been a faculty member at her middle school. Though he'd never taught her, he was the person who'd sworn the whole class into the Three Youth League when Mother had just entered the school. Mother had never considered him an acquaintance or a friend because he'd been an adult and she'd been a student. Someone had given Hu Liang's name as the person who'd recruited many young Three Youth Leaguers for the Kuomintang. This activity made him a historical counter-revolutionary.

Mother's case was now closed, and the interrogation group was dissolved. A military representative announced in a department-wide meeting that enough "evidence" had shown that Mother was indeed a historical counter-revolutionary. The military men and the revolutionary committee would decide what to do with her after the Chinese New Year.

Mother's heart was broken, and when she told me the news, she cried. I watched with horror as tears silently streamed down her face. It was the first time I'd seen her cry. In the nationwide hysteria, Mother's laughter, her smile, and her upbeat personality gave me a sense of safety and security. She was my protection and, in a way, my whole world. Now I watched as my world crumbled. I was devastated. I was afraid I would never see Mother's beautiful smile again.

I cried with her.

Father's letters stopped soon after he returned to Qinghai. We didn't know what had happened to him and didn't know where to find him. Because of the nature of his work, we were only given a post office box address so that we could write to him. But our letters were not answered or returned for weeks.

One cold afternoon, I waited in front of our apartment building for the mailman to come, as I often did.

It was winter break, and school was out. The frigid air sneaked into my cotton-padded jacket through the collar and sleeves. To keep myself warm, I tied a chain of hundreds of rubber bands to two small poplar trees and danced and skipped over it. It was a gray world: the gray sky, the gray brick buildings, the gray roads, and the gray trunks of the poplar trees.

As I played, my eyes were glued to the corner of our apartment building.

As soon as the mailman turned the corner, I ran to him and watched as he took out newspapers and letters from the big green canvas bag tied to the front of his bicycle. My heart pounded. *Today is the day,* I thought. *Look at the stack of letters in his hand; there's got to be one from Father.* I imagined giving the letter to Mother when she came home from work. "Look," I would say to her, "a letter from Dad!" I could see her smile. But all the letters went into our neighbors' mailboxes installed at the entrance of our apartment building, not ours. The mailman's hands were empty. He looked at me and shook his head. In his eyes, I saw pity. He hopped on his bicycle and rode off toward the next apartment building, leaving behind only the sound of the bicycle bell.

I walked back to the rubber-band rope. I dreaded the thought of having to tell Mother that there were still no letters from Father.

A woman's piercing voice came from the loudspeakers located on the roof of a building nearby: "Revolution is not like having a dinner banquet, writing an article, painting, or doing needlework. Revolution is violent; it is a violent act of one class overthrowing another class." It was a famous quotation from Mao. Following the woman's voice was the sound of a bugle call, signaling the opening of the campus cafeterias for dinner.

I struggled to untie the rubber-band rope from the trees. The knots were too tight, and my fingers were red and stiff from the cold weather. Frustrated, I yanked the rope off the tree, breaking it. I started to cry.

Walking through the dark hallway, I came to Mother's room and sat down at the edge of the bed by the window. On Mother's desk was a black-and-white photo sandwiched between two pieces of glass on a metal stand. Mother had taken the photo when Father had visited us in Beijing not long ago.

In the photo, Father and I were sitting in a rowboat in Kunming Lake of the Summer Palace. We both had cotton-padded jackets and wide-legged pants on. Skinny as a bird, I'd squeezed myself between Father and the side of the boat. I was laughing, unaware of the grave situation that he was in. Father looked into the distance and seemed to have a heavy heart. In the photo, a pen stuck out from the upper pocket on the left-hand side of his jacket. It was a time when being illiterate was considered glorious and being educated was "reactionary." A genuine person, Father never felt the need to hide who he was, even during the Cultural Revolution.

I couldn't recall anything alarming about Father's visit. By now, the Cultural Revolution had completely engulfed the whole nation. It had changed people in different ways: some people used every opportunity to express their exaggerated admiration toward Mao and his Cultural Revolution, while others tried desperately to avoid being persecuted as "people's enemies." But in my eyes, Father hadn't changed. He was still the calm and patient person I remembered.

The door opened. Mother came home, bringing in with her cold air and the scent of winter. Her cheeks were red from the cold. She unwrapped her long cream-colored scarf from her neck.

"I just came back from your Aunt Yue's," she said. Aunt Yue was a teacher at the university, and her husband was Father's colleague in Qinghai.

"And?" I asked, taking her black tote bag from her hand.

"Her husband's letters stopped quite a while ago, also," Mother said. "Your dad's other two colleagues haven't written to their families, either."

Father was not the only person at the university who

had been ordered to Qinghai by the government to carry out the secret mission; three other chemistry teachers had joined Father at Factory 221 and left their families behind in Beijing.

Mother seemed to be encouraged by the news. Her eyes were bright, and she had a smile on her lips.

"You see," she said, "that means your dad doesn't have issues. He and his colleagues must be working on a secret project and are not allowed to write to us."

While waiting for Father's letters, the dreaded thought that maybe he was being persecuted crept into my mind from time to time, but I never told Mother about it, and she hadn't told me that she had the same fear until now.

"That's right. Father has no issues!" I shouted. I held Mother's arms and jumped up and down.

"Silly girl," Mother said, balancing herself while smiling.

CHAPTER FIVE

1970

The morning of New Year's Eve, I woke up and looked out of the window. Bare branches of poplar trees pointed at the gloomy gray sky. It was a cold day, not windy or snowy, but dry and frigid. The lower part of the windowpane was covered with ice. Mother was already up; I could hear her making breakfast in the kitchen. I didn't get up. The radiator in the room was never warm enough, and I could feel the cold air on my face. I tucked the quilt under my chin to prevent cold air from getting in.

The Chinese New Year was the time for the whole family to be together. No matter how far away one was from home or how little money one had, New Year was the time to go home and be with loved ones, but this Chinese New Year was different. No one from my family would come back for the New Year. We still hadn't heard anything from Father. Big

Brother was not allowed to leave the border area because of the military conflict between the Soviet Union and China. He and other youths had to prepare for war. The only person who might be able to come home was Second Brother.

When the New Year was near, however, we received a letter from Second Brother. Just when the sent-down youths had been ready to buy train tickets to Beijing for the Chinese New Year, the village head had announced in a meeting: "Every year, we take a few days off during the Chinese New Year, but not this year. This year, we are going to have a revolutionized New Year. We will not take one day off."

"But there is nothing to do in the field at this time. What do we do here?" the city youths protested.

"We study," the village head replied. "We read newspapers. We study the articles by the Central Committee."

When Mother and I read Second Brother's letter, we were more than disappointed. Mother sent a letter to Second Brother telling him not to worry if he could not come home for the New Year. He might as well save his vacation for the next time our family could be together.

"Get up. We are going to make dumplings after breakfast," Mother said as she walked into my room. It was our family tradition to make dumplings for the Chinese New Year.

After breakfast, we started making ground pork and Chinese leek dumplings, my favorite kind. In our family, making dumplings was an event for the whole family. It was fun, like a party. My brothers would tell jokes, and everyone would laugh. We had Mother's laugh, loud and wholehearted. We would not hear Father laughing, though, because he was rarely with us. Even if he were there, he would not laugh out loud as we did. A calm and quiet person, he would just smile and watch his favorite people having a good time.

On this chilly New Year's Eve day, it was just Mother and me, making dumplings in silence as if we were working on a science project. After the dumplings had been made, we took them to the kitchen to be boiled. A big aluminum pot sat on a coal-burning stove in front of the window. Mother stood by the stove. I leaned on the door frame behind her. To prevent the dumplings from sticking to the bottom of the pot, Mother used a big ladle to stir them occasionally. Every now and then, she would look out the window as if she were still waiting for someone to come.

I heard a noise behind me. Mother turned around; her eyes looked beyond me, and her mouth was open. She looked surprised. I turned around and saw Second Brother standing behind me. Carrying only a small bag on his shoulder, he looked as if he had just come back from school for lunch on a regular school day.

"Mom, I'm home," he said. He stood there, tall and proud, like a soldier reporting to his commander. A big brown winter hat covered half of his face. His smile was restrained, but his eyes were sparkling. Mother and I were overjoyed.

"We thought you were not coming," Mother said. "Did your village head finally allow you to come back?"

"No. I ran away," Second Brother said. "The locals did not know I was leaving. That's why I didn't bring anything home."

Second Brother's visit brought much-needed joy to Mother and me during that cold holiday; however, we worried that he would be punished for running away when he went back to the countryside. He wasn't, though. There were no military representatives in his village to lead the witch hunt, and most villagers were not as interested in the political movement as the people in Beijing; they'd rather tend their vegetables and animals than have a rally condemning someone who'd gone back home for the holiday.

After the Chinese New Year, punishment came for Mother. She was sent to a steel factory on the outskirts of Beijing. "It could have been a lot worse," a military man said in a department-wide meeting. According to him, Mother was being treated with leniency. "The contradiction between her and the people is 'a contradiction between the people and a class enemy,'" he said. "However, we treated it as 'a contradiction among the people.'"

Mother didn't mind working as a steelworker. After the lengthy investigation, she wanted to leave the campus. She didn't want to be with the people who made her suffer and treated her like an outcast. However, she was concerned about me. Second Brother had gone back to Yunnan. To work outside Beijing, Mother would have to leave me at home by myself. I was almost 12 and knew how to cook simple meals, but she was concerned about my safety and didn't want me to feel lonely. Grandma Gao told Mother not to worry and that her family would take care of me.

"Behind our apartment door, we are practically one family," Grandma Gao said.

The day came when Mother had to leave for the factory. We got up early in the morning. I wanted to go to the bus stop with her, but she insisted that I go to school. She stood in the doorway of our apartment, her baggage lying next to her. It was the same kind of baggage that my brothers had when they were sent away: a quilt folded into a flat, square bundle with clothes wrapped inside it. On her feet was a pair of green sneakers.

"You are a big girl now," Mother said to me. "You need to take care of yourself. Don't skip any meals. Come home before it is dark." She held the key to our apartment with a loop made of a red cord fastened to it. I nodded. I was too sad to say anything. She put the key around my neck.

In the fourth year of the Cultural Revolution, our family of five was separated and living in four different places. Now Mother was leaving, too.

I went to school and played with friends after school on weekdays. When the cafeterias opened in the evenings, I would buy steamed buns from the chemistry department cafeteria. Sometimes I would buy a stir-fried dish. I knew how to make a simple soup. Nighttime was difficult. I was alone. I often lay in bed, staring at the white ceiling that seemed to be very far away and listening to the upstairs neighbors running across the room. I would wonder when Mother would come home and Father would write again.

It was chilly in early spring. Cold fronts came down from Siberia, sweeping away any signs of life. The poplar trees' bare branches twisted and turned in the wind, making a whistling sound. When it was too cold to play outside, I spent a lot of time in the Gaos' room.

Grandma Gao kept her north-facing room warm by hanging a thick quilt on the door and sealing off the window frames with newspaper. The radiators were only lukewarm, so Aunt Gao had brought in a stove. As a result, in the mornings, there was less ice on Grandma Gao's windowpanes than on Mother's, which were south-facing.

It was in the Gaos' room that I heard countless stories. One of her favorites was a story of five hundred ducks.

"A teacher is standing in front of the class," Grandma Gao started.

"He has a brand-new, long robe on and a mustache that makes him look very smart. Two women are chatting loudly outside the classroom window. The teacher walks out of the classroom and shushes them. He walks back and says to the students, 'When two women are together, they are as noisy as one thousand ducks.' The teacher shakes his head."

Grandma Gao took a sip from a white teacup and continued:

"The next day, someone is knocking at the classroom door, and the teacher asks a boy to check it out. The boy goes out and comes back. He reports to the teacher, 'There are five hundred ducks outside.' The teacher walks out and sees his wife. The teacher asks the boy, 'Where are the ducks?' The boy answers, 'You said that two women made one thousand ducks. Now there is only one woman.'"

By now, Grandma Gao was doubled over with laughter.

"Then what?" I asked, waiting for the ending. Grandma Gao said that the story had ended. She was laughing and slapping her thigh with her hand.

Listening to Grandma Gao's stories made me forget my loneliness. I especially liked it when she ended some stories by saying, "Bad things don't happen to good people." She would say each word clearly and stick a brown tobacco pipe into her mouth afterward as if she had just made an announcement to the whole world. I believed her. Not living with my family made me worry about them; Grandma Gao's words were reassuring.

As the nights went deeper, Grandma Gao would become tired. However, I would insist on her telling me more stories.

"One more story, Grandma," I would beg. I was afraid that once Grandma Gao ran out of stories, I would have to go back to my room. There I would be alone.

"I have no more stories," Grandma Gao would say, yawning.

"Let me tell you a story, then," I would say.

Often, before I finished my story, Grandma Gao would doze off with her back against a pile of folded quilts, legs bent in front of her and head hanging.

"Grandma, wake up. Grandma, wake up." I would pat her knee.

During the difficult time, the Gao family did many things for me that warmed my heart, but it was what they didn't do that gave me a sense of security; they never asked me to leave their room. I cannot recall one instance when Grandma Gao or Aunt Gao said to me, "Kid, go home. I am tired," and sent me out the door. They didn't want me to feel the pain of not having my family around. They treated me like their own family, as they had promised Mother.

Not everything that Grandma Gao said was lighthearted. Sometimes she would say things that scared me. One day, after fixing her hair, she sat on the bed with her legs folded in front of her. I was sitting at the edge of the bed. The water in the teapot was bubbling on the stove. The pleasant aroma from the orange peel that she'd put on top of the stove filled the air.

Suddenly, Grandma Gao said to me, "Do you know Chiang Kai-shek is actually one good-looking man?" As if to show how good-looking Chiang Kai-shek was, she straightened her back and stretched her neck. It felt as if a clap of thunder had just exploded over my head. Chiang Kai-shek was the leader of the Kuomintang and Mao's biggest enemy outside the Communist Party. At the time, saying Chiang's name without attaching degrading nicknames such as "Chiang the Baldy," "Chiang Kai-shek the people's enemy," or "Chiang who should have been dead" was showing too much respect for him. Paying compliments to his looks was suicidal.

My heart was pounding. I had never dreamed that Grandma Gao would say such a thing, although I knew she didn't agree with the government on a lot of things. For example, she didn't think the vast population was the reason that China was poor, as the government told us.

"Why is America the richest country, then, and not Mongolia?" Grandma Gao once asked me. Her son-in-law had worked in Mongolia for two years, and Grandma Gao knew that Mongolia was a desolated and impoverished nation. I didn't argue with her because I knew she didn't participate in political studies and, therefore, couldn't "keep up with the situation."

However, praising the people's number-one enemy Chiang Kai-shek? Grandma Gao was out of line. This comment alone would qualify her as a counter-revolutionary. I wanted to run out of the room so that she would stop the scary talk. Then I saw the window was closed and the gaps in the window frames were tightly sealed off with newspapers. No one else could hear Grandma Gao's speech.

I stayed and pretended I didn't hear her and hoped she would change the subject.

"Lin Biao has the look of a treacherous official," Grandma Gao said. I almost fell off the bed. It felt as if all my blood had rushed to the bottoms of my feet, and I felt lightheaded. Lin Biao was the second-highest leader, right below Mao. Saying anything against Lin Biao would be punished as severely as saying anything against Mao. I ran out of the room. As I was leaving, Grandma Gao was still offering her analysis on Lin Biao's looks: "Look at his bushy eyebrows. Look at his fleshless cheeks and his triangle eyes. Does he look like an honest man?"

∾

"You didn't come back for lunch," Grandma Gao said when I came home one afternoon. She was sitting in bed under the window. In her hands was the sole of the shoe that she was making for her grandson.

"We ate at school," I told her.

"Recalling bitterness meal?" she asked, looking at me from above her glasses.

I nodded.

The university where our school was located was surrounded by farmland. The people's communes nearby often solicited the elementary school students' help in the fields. In summer, we helped them harvest wheat, and in winter, bok choy. In return, the people's communes sent peasants to give speeches to school students about their hard lives in pre-communist China. At "recalling bitterness [in old society] and reflecting happiness [in new China]" rallies, the speakers complained about the landlords' aggressive attempts to collect sharecropping payments in the years of severe drought, leaving not enough food for them to eat. The speakers and the audience were united by the shared appreciation for the party and the hatred for the landlords. Slogans were shouted, and tears were shed. After rallies, we were often made to eat a "recalling bitterness meal." The recipe came from the peasant speakers at the rallies. The food was mainly made of cornmeal and coarsely ground wheat husks. The mix was made into balls the size of baseballs. It was a class-struggle education tool designed to show us that if it weren't for the communists, we would all be eating the kind of food poor peasants ate in old China.

Grandma Gao leaned toward the window to examine the shoe sole she had made with layers of scrap fabric bound by adhesive.

"In old China, landlords were so mean," I said. "I felt so bad for poor people then." I told Grandma Gao that I'd cried during the rally, as a lot of children did.

"My child, the life people have now is no better than before," she said, looking up from her work.

I was shocked. Growing up in a nation where only one voice was allowed, I had never heard anyone talk like this before. Even when grown-ups complained behind closed doors, they would only dare to criticize a particular party official or a specific party policy. Grandma Gao's statement challenged the legitimacy of the Chinese communist government. It was against everything I had been taught.

By now, I was old enough to sense that things in China were not as great as the government portrayed them and that people were suffering. However, I never thought that was a sufficient reason to stop supporting the government. We were told every day that the goal of the communist government was to "serve the people," and it did everything to ensure that the Chinese people would never have to endure hardship again. The government's propaganda had convinced me that life for Chinese people was better under the communists. The party's catch-all defense for its barbaric policies and ruthless control of its people was: "We may have killed a few people, but the majority of people's lives are better." Due to information control by the government, I wasn't aware that 30 to 40 million people had starved to death under Mao shortly after I was born.

My first instinct was to jump up and cover Grandma Gao's mouth with my hands, but I didn't. I calmed down and started arguing with her with what I had learned in school.

"In the old society, only rich people had money to buy things," I said.

"At least," Grandma Gao said, "back then, people could buy things with money. Now everything is rationed. Even with money, you still cannot buy what you need." She made another hole in the sole with an awl and pulled a thick white thread through it.

Grandma Gao was right. In the name of equality, the communists created a society where everyone was poor except for the high-ranking communist officials. As the Cultural Revolution progressed, more and more life necessities were rationed: rice, flour, meat, cooking oil, rice noodles, fabric, clothes, yarn, socks, cotton, and so on. At one point, a single family in Beijing could only buy 20 cents' worth of pork each day, which was a slice of pork the size of a piece of bacon. Once a year, people could buy a small amount of peanuts and sunflower seeds for the Chinese New Year.

"If back then, people had needed ration coupons to buy fabric like now," Grandma Gao said, "no one would have made new clothes, and I would not have been able to raise your Aunt Gao and send her to school with my tailoring business."

I looked at my pants. They were old, and the dark blue color had faded. There were patches on the knees and the buttocks. The legs of the pants had been extended twice. I was growing fast and needed new clothes, but we didn't have enough fabric ration coupons. When my pants became too short and the legs dangled above my ankles, Mother would say, "You look like you are going fishing. Let's add fabric to the bottom of the legs." So, we would. I'd grow taller again, and more fabric would have to be added.

As I spent more time with Grandma Gao, I grew used to her outrageous comments and stopped running away. Instead, I just listened. Although I had no reason to question her truthfulness, I chose not to believe her. I couldn't allow myself to question the government. I was a good person, and like Father, I would do important things for China when I grew up. That was my identity, and I couldn't give it up. I had to love China and support the government.

᠃

I don't remember exactly when it happened, but one day, Teacher Li came back to teach.

That morning, she walked into the classroom and stood in front of the blackboard as if nothing had happened. No one explained to us why she was allowed to teach again, and no one told us the result of the investigations.

Her appearance hadn't changed much; she still had her blue shirt on, and her face was still pale. Even her hair looked the same: it rose up in the front by at least an inch.

As I looked at Teacher Li, my feelings were complex. On the one hand, I was happy for her now that she was allowed to teach again and we were going to learn arithmetic and new Chinese characters. On the other hand, I didn't know how she felt about us. I wondered if she still trusted us or if she blamed her students for her suffering. I felt guilty when she looked at me, because I had been there at the rally where she had been assaulted. She must have thought that all the students had been there to humiliate her that day.

"Call me Platoon Leader Li from now on," she said to the class.

Making students march was not enough; the military representatives ordered the school to adopt the military ranking system. In the system, each class became a platoon. Three classes made a company, where one teacher became a company commander and another teacher became a political adviser. In the real military, the company commander would lead a company in battle while the company's political adviser was in charge of the people's thoughts. Of course, the teachers were not real military people. They were still civilians wearing civilian clothes.

On April 24, China launched its first satellite, named Red East I. It was another big event that the government claimed to be "a huge blow to our enemies, especially the American imperialists." According to the media, the music of "The East Is Red" was blasted out into space from the satellite. We sang the song every day and knew the lyrics well: "The East is red, the sun rises, and China has Mao Zedong." On the night of the big news, people rushed to the streets, cheering and celebrating. The next day, the school canceled classes so that we could continue celebrating. We walked to a nearby elementary school to join a giant mass rally with 11 other elementary schools.

Following an hours-long rally and many speeches, there was a parade. Mao's portraits, red banners, and red flags flooded the streets. Everywhere I looked, I saw black hair and red flags. During the parade, Teacher Li ran up from behind and caught up with me. Her usually pale face was pink from running, and she had a big smile on her face.

Teacher Li and I walked side by side. With each step, her dark hair bounced on her shoulders. We smiled at each other, and we held our heads high. We were proud of the fact that now China had a satellite.

"Have you heard from your father?" Teacher Li asked me.

"Not yet," I said. I was surprised she knew that we hadn't

received letters from Father for months. I hadn't told anyone about it. She must have heard it from the families of Father's colleagues.

"Now that the satellite has been launched, you are going to hear from your father soon," she said. Her eyes filled with warmth, and she nodded at me as if to say, "Trust me; I know it." I noticed that she had fine wrinkles at the corners of her eyes that I hadn't seen before.

When Mother came back from the steel factory for her monthly visit, I asked her, "Is my father making satellites?"

"No," Mother said.

Teacher Li was wrong. I was disappointed.

"Your father is doing something very important for China," Mother said. I saw the familiar glow on her face when she talked about Father. I didn't ask her what Father was doing because I knew I wasn't supposed to know, but I felt proud. I told myself that one day, I would do something important for China, too.

The military men left our school after they picked five trusted people, one previous school official and four teachers, to form a revolutionary committee, replacing the old school authority.

After half a year of working in the steel factory, Mother was called back to the university by the revolutionary committee of the department. This occurred after she'd made numerous requests. She didn't want me to live by myself for too long.

The physical labor, however, continued for her.

First, she made bricks for air-raid shelters on campus, and then she worked as a plumber. Once, I saw Mother and a male counter-revolutionary in her department carrying a piece of timber bamboo on their shoulders as they walked across campus. When I got closer, I recognized the man as Lan, who had kneeled in front of Mao's portrait. Mother and Lan both wore faded blue clothes and old blue hats. The bamboo was at least 20 feet long and cut lengthwise. Mother carried one end in the front, and Lan carried the other end in the back. The bamboo was bouncing up and down on their shoulders as they walked. I ran over to Mother and wanted to carry the bamboo for her, but she stepped sideways to avoid me.

"Go away," she said. "Go play with your friends." Her voice was stern. I later learned that the piece of bamboo was used to unplug sewer lines.

After working on the main sewer lines for a few weeks, Mother was sent to raise pigs for the campus cafeterias. Meat was in shortage. Every department raised pigs for its cafeterias. It was a punishment because raising pigs was considered menial and degrading. Mother didn't mind because pigs didn't discriminate. They had no hatred toward a counter-revolutionary. Besides, Mother learned something from the pig-raising experience.

"I did it all wrong with you all these years," Mother said to me after studying me for a while at the dinner table one evening. "The reason pigs grow so fast is that, at each meal, they are fed soup first; this way, their stomachs are enlarged so that they can eat more." She studied my face. "Look how skinny you are. Your ears are so thin that they are transparent. Light can shine through them." She shook her head. "From now on, you should have soup before every meal." I was delighted. Before that, Mother would not allow water on the dining table, and I could only have soup at the very end of the meals because she was afraid water and soups would dilute the gastric juice in our stomachs.

It was a difficult time in our lives. We still hadn't heard from Father, and my brothers were far away. Mother was labeled a class enemy and forced to do hard labor. Nevertheless, she and I were together again. We supported and comforted each other. We believed that together we could survive anything. Our little apartment was our refuge.

One evening, a young teacher from the university came to visit. His name was Wang. He was pale, thin, and wearing glasses. In his arms was a beautiful baby girl. After Wang had settled in a chair next to a desk in Mother's room, he told us that he was going to Qinghai. Mother poured a cup of jasmine flower tea for him before she sat down at the desk.

Wang's wife had been Father's colleague at the university, and they were working together again at Factory

221. Wang hadn't heard from his wife for months, so he'd decided to make a trip to Qinghai to see her. He was not being persecuted or under investigation and was able to get permission from the revolutionary committee at the university to leave Beijing.

"I will send my wife a telegram asking her to meet us at the Xining train station when our train arrives," Wang said. Like our family, he only had his wife's post office box address. "I will take our daughter with me."

"It will be a long train ride," Mother said, looking at the little girl who was playing with the buttons on Wang's shirt.

"Our daughter needs to see her mother," he said, and then he put the little girl's hand in his mouth, pretending he was biting her. She giggled, showing two lower teeth. "I will be back by the end of the month," he said before taking off with his daughter.

Wang and his daughter visited us again much sooner than expected. It turned out that after the long train ride, they had arrived at Xining, the capital of Qinghai province. At the train station, instead of his wife, Wang was met by two men in military uniforms who claimed to be the military representatives at Factory 221. The military men told Wang that Factory 221 was under martial law and no one was allowed to contact anybody outside. They asked Wang to go back to Beijing.

"But I haven't seen my wife yet," Wang said. "Can I at least see her here at the train station? Our daughter needs to see her mother."

"She is not coming, and you are not going to see her,"

one of the military men said to Wang. "No one is allowed to interfere with the Cultural Revolution. You are not allowed to stay. You must leave immediately."

Wang and his baby girl hadn't even stepped out of the train station before they were put on the next train back to Beijing.

Wang frowned the whole time he talked. The room fell into dead silence after he finished his story. There was nothing else to say and nothing else to do.

CHAPTER SIX

1971

It was a few days before summer break, my last year in elementary school. I was 13.

In the middle of the Cultural Revolution, the city government had ordered the school year to start in spring instead of fall. I suspected this was an effort to get rid of old rules and traditions. As a result, I spent six and a half years in elementary school instead of six.

Lunch break was almost over; Mother was still not home. Worried, I looked out the window. Everything was white under the glaring sun. I looked at the narrow road Mother walked along to go to work each morning. It stretched south from our apartment to the gray campus clinic building about a hundred yards away. There it turned into a wide asphalt street and wrapped around the building before continuing.

Many mornings, through the window, I watched

as Mother followed the road to the clinic building and disappeared behind it only to reappear a few minutes later and walk on. And in the evenings, my eyes often found her walking down the road on her way home after a day's work. When she got closer, she would look up at our window, and my heart would race as I rushed to the door.

Now the road was empty. The vacant land between our building and the campus clinic was littered with broken bricks and scarred with holes and ditches. The barren land looked tired and downtrodden, like the people and the nation after five years of turmoil brought on by the Cultural Revolution. The gray wall of the campus clinic building was covered with big-character posters. The once brightly colored posters had faded. Some were torn, and long strips of paper dangled from the wall. It was a solemn world; even the cicadas had stopped singing.

I went to the kitchen and started preparing lunch.

We had no refrigerator. To prevent food from being spoiled, we heated up the leftover food the night before and kept it in a small burgundy-colored kitchen cabinet. I put two steamed buns and a stir-fried vegetable dish in a dented old aluminum steamer and set it on a coal-burning stove. Soon the steamer made a hissing sound. The water was boiling. I set two bowls and two pairs of chopsticks on the dining table in my room where we usually ate. I then sat down. The room was quiet; the only sound came from an alarm clock standing on a yellow dresser. Each time the thin arm moved, it made a distinct sound: tick-tock.

When Mother finally came home, she walked through

the hallway and disappeared into her room without saying a word. *She must be really tired from work,* I thought. Concerned, I walked to her room, pushed open the door, and saw her sitting in a bamboo armchair in front of the south-facing window. Usually, she would take off her faded blue work shirt as soon as she came home and put on clean, comfortable clothes, but not today. She stared at the empty wall with her work shirt still on. Hearing me come into the room, she turned to me. She had a blank look on her face.

"A military representative in the department told me not to go back to work after lunch," she said. "He wants to come here to talk to me this afternoon." She looked at me, but it felt as if she didn't see me. She had a faraway look on her face.

"Why?" I asked. The military men had never come to our home before, even when they'd sent Mother away to work at the steel factory. They had simply told her in the office that she needed to pack right away. I worried that they were sending her even farther away this time.

Mother didn't answer me.

Bright sunlight poured in from the window behind her, leaving her face in the shadow. I walked closer and stood by her.

"What does the military man want to talk about?" I asked.

"He wouldn't tell me," Mother said, looking at me and pausing for a few seconds. "I am afraid it is about your father." When she mentioned him, her voice became soft, and her eyes drifted away from my face.

My heart skipped a beat. I grabbed Mother's chair by the armrest. "I want to stay home and hear what the military man has to say."

"No, you need to go to school," she said. I was startled by her harsh tone and let go of the armrest. Mother sank deeper into the armchair.

"Something has happened to your father," she said after a brief silence, softening her voice. In fact, her voice was so low that she was almost whispering.

"What do you mean, 'something has happened'?" I asked nervously in a raspy voice.

"I saw the way some of my colleagues looked at me today," Mother said. Slouching in the armchair, she looked drained. "Their eyes were filled with pity. They must have heard something. Something bad has happened to your father."

Although Mother's voice was soft, I heard her words loud and clear like thunder on a quiet night. My heart was sinking.

"Maybe the military representative wants to talk about your work," I said.

"Why wouldn't he talk to me in the office, then?" she asked. "Obviously, he didn't want me to make a scene." In her eyes, I saw something that I had never seen in her before: panic.

I searched for the right words to convince her that Father was all right, but I couldn't find any. I felt inadequate. I would say or do anything to make her worries go away, but I didn't know how. I wished my brothers were home. They might have known what to say.

Mother buried her face in her hands.

I stood by her, not knowing what else to say.

Outside the window, a Persian silk tree was just tall enough to lift its flowering branches above the sill. The pink and fragrant flowers were light like clouds and soft like a dream. During the three years of famine from 1959 to 1961 caused by the Great Leap Forward Movement, not only were peasants starving, but even city people didn't have enough to eat. Food was rationed. To compensate for the food shortage, the university divided the land around the apartment buildings into small plots and allowed each family to have one plot to grow food. At the time, Father was still working in Beijing and attended to the garden regularly. According to Mother, our garden was the envy of the neighbors; the vegetables were big, and the flowers beautiful. I believed it was Father who had planted the Persian silk tree outside our window.

The tree has a beautiful Chinese name, He Huan, which means "companion." Some say the name is from the fact that the leaves of the tree grow in pairs and they close every night like lovers embracing each other. Others say the name came from an ancient Chinese love story:

> *Long ago, He Huan did not flower, and the name was not He Huan, either. It was called Ku Qing, meaning "grief." One day, a young woman saw her husband off to take imperial exams in the capital. It was a long way from home; there were mountains and rivers on the way. It could be months or even years before the husband would return home. Before the*

husband left for his journey, the wife took him to Ku Qing, the tree that had never blossomed. "I will always wait for you faithfully," she said. "Rain or shine, sunrise or sundown, I will wait for you like this tree."

The husband left and never returned. The wife waited and waited. Years passed, and the woman was sick and dying. At the very last moment of her life, she struggled to the tree and made a wish: she wanted to become the flowers of the tree, and her husband the green leaves. That way, they would be together until the end of the world. The wife died. The next summer, the tree blossomed for the first time. The pink and fragrant flowers covered the branches, light like clouds, soft like a dream. The tree bloomed every year from then on. No one called the tree "grief" anymore. The tree had a new name: He Huan—companion.

Mother insisted that I go to school after lunch. While I was there, my mind was home with Mother. Unlike her, I didn't believe anything bad could happen to Father. I couldn't imagine the worst. Time stood still, and I couldn't wait for school to be over. Finally, the bell rang. I dashed out of the classroom and ran all the way home.

I walked through the dark, narrow hallway, passing our neighbor's room, and came to Mother's room. I opened the door.

The room was filled with thick cigarette smoke. Through the eye-watering, suffocating haze, I saw not one, but a roomful of military men sitting in the chairs randomly scattered about. They all wore green military uniforms and had a cigarette in hand. At the far end of the room, under the window, Mother was sitting in her armchair, still in the blue shirt. Her eyes were puffy. She had been crying. Hearing the door, everyone in the room turned their heads and looked at me. No one moved or said anything. I stood by the door, frozen.

Someone grabbed my arm from behind. I turned around. It was our neighbor Aunt Gao. She had tears in her eyes. She pulled me away from Mother's door and led me to her room. Grandma Gao was standing by the door. She took me inside by my hands. They must have heard me when I came home.

Grandma Gao struggled to get the words out. "Hai zi," she said. She always called me Hai zi, Chinese for "child." "Your father is gone."

I looked at Grandma Gao and couldn't believe the horrible words that came out from her mouth. When Mother had told me that she feared something bad had happened to Father, not only had I refused to think what that "something bad" could have been, but even if I had thought about it, I would never have considered the possibility that Father could be dead. I was in disbelief, but the grim look on Grandma Gao's face told me that I'd heard her right; Father was dead. I started to cry. Tears rolled down my face, wetting my shirt.

"Hai Zi," Grandma Gao called to me. I lifted my head.

Through tears, I saw her blurry face. "If you want to say something, you should say it." She handed me a handkerchief. "Don't keep it inside; cry out loud."

I nodded but said nothing. The bad news had hit me so hard that it had crushed me. *This is awful. It isn't supposed to happen,* I said to myself. The thought repeated itself in my head like a broken record. It was the only thing I could think of. I couldn't believe that Father, the kind and humble man, the man who used to tell me bedtime stories during his annual trips back to Beijing, the man who called me "the tiniest" when I was younger, the man who always asked my brothers and me to help Mother with the household chores in his letters, and the man for whom we'd waited in agony for almost two years, would never come home.

Grandma Gao and her daughter sat by my side at the edge of the bed and wept, though they had only known Father for a short time. About three years earlier, when Father had come home for his annual vacation, he had brought yarn from Qinghai province as a gift for the Gao family, the new neighbors he had not met. Qinghai was known for its good-quality yarn. The Gao family had been moved by Father's gesture. Before meeting him, they'd been worried about how Father would treat them; after all, we had been forced by armed revolutionaries to accept the Gao family into our apartment. Grandma Gao often mentioned what a kind person Father was. "A real gentleman," she would say. Now they were saddened by his passing.

"Let them have a horrible death," Grandma Gao said under her breath. "Let lightning strike them!" She was cussing at the military men.

My mind went numb, and my head was empty. I was not in the mindset to think about why Father had died and who was responsible for his death. All I knew was that the unthinkable had happened; there would never be letters in light blue envelopes that put a smile on Mother's face, and there would never be trips to the Summer Palace with Father. He would never call me "the tiniest," smiling and tilting his head to the side, with sunlight pouring in through the window behind him, on his hair and on his shoulders.

I finally cried out loud.

I went into Mother's room after the military people had left. The smoke from their cigarettes was still thick. The sun had set, and the room was dark. I couldn't see where Mother was. I searched for the light switch on the wall by the door with my hand.

"No. Don't turn on the light," Mother said. She was lying in bed. A strong and independent woman, Mother had never let anything defeat her. No matter how difficult things were, her laughter was never absent for long. She was able to walk out of the door with her head held high even after she was labeled a class enemy not only because of her upbeat personality but also because of Father's love. He believed in her and loved her, but now Father was gone. Mother had lost the love of her life. The news devastated her.

The Gao family was quiet. The loudspeakers on campus went silent after blasting out the sound of the last bugle call of the day. Even the family above us didn't run around as they always did. Usually, Aunt Gao's son, Little Red Moon, would come over as soon as he heard Mother or me come home. He would push open our door and then stand there with a big smile on his face. He didn't show up today. Grandma Gao must have forbidden him from bothering Mother.

The stillness of the night made me wonder if what had happened earlier was just a nightmare. Father hadn't died. He would come home one day like other children's fathers. We would row boats in the Summer Palace. We would go to the Beijing Observatory and watch the giant pendulum swinging back and forth. We would go to the Beijing Zoo and listen to the birds singing and watch giraffes drinking water. However, the lingering smell of the cigarettes told me that the military men had come and delivered the heartbreaking news. I started sobbing.

I heard Mother calling my name. "We need to be strong," she said. I wiped the tears from my face, waiting for her to say more. I didn't know what being strong meant.

Mother sat up on the bed. She told me that the people I had seen in the afternoon were military representatives; some were from the chemistry department where Mother worked, and some were from Factory 221. "Your husband is dead," a military man from Factory 221 had told Mother. "He died of chronic pancreatitis more than a year ago. His body has already been cremated. We brought his ashes with us." The military men wanted to drop off the ashes and head back to Qinghai.

Words couldn't describe how shocked and outraged I was.

Mother and I had waited for 20 months from the day Father's letters stopped to the day we were notified of his death; we hadn't known that he was already gone. Mother was furious. She didn't know how Father had died, but she did know that he had not died from an illness. The military men were covering up their crimes.

"If you cooperate with us and accept the ashes," one military man had said, "your husband's death will be treated as death on duty, which means there will be monetary compensation to your family." It was customary in China that accepting the ashes meant the family was not suspicious of the cause of death and was satisfied with the handling of the death by the government. In other words, the family was willing to settle, and the case was closed.

"Take the ashes and go away," Mother had said. "What 'death on duty'? What duty?!" She was enraged. "Until you tell me the truth about my husband's death, I will not accept the ashes."

Realizing that Mother could not be intimidated, the military men had smoked incessantly.

The Gao family brought us dinner on a bamboo tray: two steamed buns and soup. But neither Mother nor I could eat.

That night, I lay in bed and tried hard not to think about what had happened during the day. I told myself that I mustn't cry. If I didn't cry, then the bad thing hadn't happened to Father. However, as hard as I tried not to cry, tears soaked my pillow. In the back of my mind, I knew the hope that Father was still alive was very slim.

The next morning, I went to school as if nothing had happened. I believed that if I kept everything the same, nothing would change. Father would still be alive, and one day, he would come home. Mother didn't stop me when I went to school, though she didn't go to work herself.

Rumors spread in the university. Friends told me that they had heard Father hadn't died; instead, he'd been abducted by the Russians or Americans. I welcomed those rumors because they gave me a glimmer of hope that Father was still alive.

Father's death became more real when my brothers came home from the countryside. The telegrams sent by Mother's colleagues brought them back. The telegrams were essential for my brothers to get permission to leave their villages. I had denied the fact that Father was dead for as long as I could, but seeing my brothers at home forced me to accept the reality: Father was gone, and from now on, there would just be four of us.

Big Brother came back to Beijing first. Not wanting people to hear him crying, he sat in bed and covered his head with a quilt. He cried the whole afternoon. The next day, Second Brother came back, but he didn't cry. I had never seen him cry.

Mother gathered the three of us. She made us sit in her room, the same room where we had read Father's letters together in the past.

"All these years," Mother said, "your father and I were not allowed to tell you children this, but I guess now it doesn't matter anymore." She paused for a second and then continued. "Your father was making atomic bombs for China."

My mouth was open for a long time. I'd had no idea that Father had been working on the bomb.

To the Chinese, a nuclear bomb was much more than just a weapon. It was a source of the Chinese people's pride. Though we could not buy food or clothing without ration coupons or travel without permission, we had the bomb. In the Chinese people's minds, having nuclear weapons elevated China's status above all the countries that didn't have them. In a country where the government stripped everything from the people—freedom, dignity, hope, property, opportunity, and even self-identity—we hung on to the only thing that the government allowed us to have: national pride. At the time, we didn't know that the bomb belonged to Mao and the Chinese government, not the Chinese people.

"An atomic bomb needs high explosives to detonate it," Mother said. "In early 1960, a team of 30 people was assembled to work on chemical explosives to detonate the bomb, but they had no luck. The government then summoned your father to join the nuclear weapons research program because he was an explosives expert."

According to Mother, Father was first sent to Xi'an and then, a year later, to Qinghai. Father and his colleagues perfected the formula for chemical explosives, conducted thousands of tests of synchronization of the explosives, and eventually succeeded in making high explosives and electric spark detonators that detonated China's first bomb.

Father was made the director of the Second Production Division, a division focused on researching and producing explosives used to detonate atomic bombs. It was also responsible for the final assembly of the bombs.

If I had heard this when Father was alive, I would have

been very proud, but now Father was dead; as Mother had said, all this didn't matter anymore.

"If Dad didn't go to Qinghai to work on the bomb, he would still be alive," I said, trying to control the quaver in my voice.

Mother sighed. "You are so naïve," she said. "Your father didn't receive an invitation from the government. He received an order from the State Council commanding him to report to the Second Ministry of Machinery Industry." Her eyes closed briefly. "Your father made a great contribution to the country; the country needs to give him justice."

After a short stay at home, my brothers left Beijing, left Mother and me, left a home that was broken forever, and went back to the countryside to continue their "re-education."

After my brothers left, I found an envelope under Second Brother's pillow; inside was a piece of paper. It was wrinkled. Someone had crumpled it, then smoothed it out, and then put it back in the envelope. It was the telegram that had delivered the heartbreaking news of Father's death to Second Brother. Evidently, the paper had been wet at one time, because it had lost its smoothness. Four characters in blue ink were smeared and blurry. However, I was able to recognize the four cold and merciless characters: "Father died. Come home."

That summer, Mother worked many Sundays so that she could take at least one weekday off per week to visit the government officials. This was the only way to find out how Father had died because, at the time, there were no lawyers, no police, and no independent judicial system. Mao's words and the party's policies were the law. Mother and I started out at the lowest level, the Ninth Academy (Qinghai-based Nuclear Weapons Research and Design Academy) in the Second Ministry of Machinery Industry, to which Factory 221 belonged. Each time we didn't get anyone to listen to us, we went one level up. When the Ninth Academy didn't respond, we went to the Second Ministry of Machinery Industry, the Ministry of Public Safety, and eventually the State Council.

When we visited the government entities, we were stopped at the gates of the compounds. Like the university, each government compound had walls around it, only the walls around the government compounds were taller and the guards were armed soldiers instead of civilians. At the reception offices outside the gates of the government compounds, Mother and I stated our request to see the officials. Each time, we received the same answer.

"No. The officials cannot see you. Why don't you leave your petition with us, and we will deliver it for you?"

"When are we going to hear an answer?" Mother asked.

"I don't know."

Usually, this was the time when the receptionists started getting impatient. Father's death didn't give them any reason for sympathy. Anyone who died during the Cultural Revolution was automatically assumed to be a class enemy. Mother and I were never allowed to enter any government compounds, and we never heard a word from any officials.

In the evenings, we wrote letters to Premier Zhou Enlai and Lin Biao, vice-chairman of the party, as well as Mao. However, our letters and requests received no response.

One hot day, Mother and I got up early and took two buses to the State Council, the highest administrative office in China. We had been here before and left our petition but had not heard anything. So, we came back. Once again, Mother and I were stopped at the gate of the compound, which was enclosed by tall gray concrete walls.

"The government officials handle 10,000 urgent issues a day," a female receptionist in the reception office at the gate said. "They cannot see you."

"It was the State Council that ordered my husband to work for the Second Ministry of Machinery Industry," Mother said. "Now he is dead. It is not too much to ask the State Council to investigate and tell us the truth."

The receptionist didn't even lift her eyelids.

We had no choice but to leave. As we walked away, I looked back at the walls, feeling helpless. I used to feel safe and privileged behind the walls of the university. The peasants outside the walls were not allowed to enter the campus unless they came to deliver vegetables. They were on the wrong side of the walls. Now, seeking justice for Father, Mother and I were on the wrong side.

At the end of the disappointing day, Mother and I headed home. She looked tired. On the hot and crowded bus, she struggled to hang on to a vertical handlebar with both hands. She stared aimlessly out of the bus window, and her lips were tightly closed. We didn't say anything during the bus ride. The silence continued as we walked home. The asphalt road from the bus station to the gate of our residential area was sandwiched between two walls; on the left was the university, and on the right was a hotel. Walking on the mile-long road that seemed endless, I was tired and angry.

My mind wandered. Memory took me back a few years to a time before the Cultural Revolution, a time when the road wasn't this quiet and the mood of people not this somber. Instead of a wall, there was a fence on the campus side, and inside it was an apple orchard. It was springtime, and I was still in kindergarten. Father was on his vacation in Beijing. Father, Mother, and I were on our way home from visiting Father's parents in another part of the city. In my mind's eye, I saw Mother laughing, Father smiling, and the apple trees blooming. The beautiful white flowers with a pink tint reached out from behind the green fence. Soft and fragile, they put on a passionate display. I was wearing my favorite red jacket with a yellow pocket in the front. The pocket was in the shape of a duck that had a big, flat beak. I ran in front of my parents and lifted my arm to touch the flowers with my fingertips.

"Aren't you tired after running around the whole day?"

Mother asked from behind me.

"Let her run," Father said.

Encouraged, I ran even faster. I stopped when I ran out of breath. I turned around.

"Dad, Mom, hurry up." I waved my arms at my parents. They looked at each other and smiled. Father waved back.

"Carry me, Dad. I'm really tired," I said when they caught up with me.

"You were just running minutes ago," Mother said, smiling. "Now you're tired?"

Father bent over and picked me up. I was happy to be in his arms.

That was a few years ago. Now Father was gone, and Mother and I were walking on the same road after another failed attempt to find justice for him. The memory was so sweet yet so painful. My parents would never walk down the road side by side, and Father would never be there to pick me up when I was tired and beaten down by life.

The communist propaganda machine described the bleak existence of the Chinese people in old China as "crying out to the heavens, but the heavens don't respond; crying out to the earth, but the earth is impervious." The expression accurately described the sense of desperation that I felt at that moment.

As sad and angry as I was, I didn't know I should direct the anger at Mao and his party. I'd never heard anyone ever question, let alone criticize, the government. Even Grandma Gao, who was the most outspoken person I'd known, would start her sentences by saying, "Chairman Mao is good

Chairman Mao; it is just the officials below him who do all the bad things."

The setting sun had lost its luster, but my eyes were burning. I closed my eyes; tears streamed down. I wiped them off with the back of my hand.

"Don't cry," Mother said, handing me a handkerchief.

"I never did anything for my father, and now we cannot even find out what happened to him," I said.

Mother slowed down and turned her face to me. I was surprised to see the light in her eyes and a smile on her face. That light had dimmed the day she'd heard the news of Father's passing, but now it had reappeared.

"Who said you haven't done anything for your father?" she asked. "Don't you know how happy he was when you were born?"

It was a story Mother had told me before. After two sons, Father wanted a little girl. When Mother gave birth to me in the hospital, a nurse called Father at work.

"Is it a girl?" Father asked.

"I will not tell you over the phone," the nurse teased. When Father rushed over to the hospital and learned that he had a new daughter, he was delighted.

He picked me up. "Isn't she the tiniest?" he said to Mother.

From then on, "the tiniest" became my nickname. The pronunciation was in an old Beijing dialect and a tongue twister. Only Father, who had grown up in old Beijing, felt comfortable saying it, so "the tiniest" became a nickname only Father used. To welcome Mother and me home from the hospital, Father decorated one room in our apartment for us. When I arrived at home for the first time, waiting for us on two white nightstands on each side of the bed were beautiful white peonies in white vases.

I was born in springtime, when the air in Beijing was still cold. That year, many newborns died from pneumonia. When I was 40 days old, I caught pneumonia and was hospitalized with a high fever. With too many sick babies, the doctors and nurses were swamped and asked one of my parents to stay in the hospital with me. In China, the role of nurse's assistant, and sometimes even of nurse, was played by family members of the patients. Father stayed in the hospital with me day and night. During my stay, he had a middle ear infection, but he didn't rest or seek treatment. He had found out that a daughter of his colleague had just passed away from pneumonia in the same hospital. The news made him worry about me even more. Even though we were in a hospital, he didn't want to leave me to see a doctor for his condition, which was worsening. He was afraid that I would suddenly turn blue and die like his colleague's child had. Eventually I survived pneumonia and went home, but Father didn't receive prompt treatment and suffered permanent hearing loss in his left ear.

I was eager to grow up. When I was five or six years old, I tracked my height using a tabletop. One day, I stood on my toes and was able to put my chin on the glass top of the bamboo table for the first time. I was excited. *I am a big girl now,* I thought. That year, when Father came home to visit, he called me "the tiniest" again. I dragged him to the table by his hand and showed him that I was taller than the table.

He smiled and picked me up. He said, "One day, you will be all grown, and I will not be able to pick you up anymore. Until then, you are still my tiniest."

❧

October 1, the anniversary of the day Mao had been crowned 22 years earlier, was celebrated as the biggest national holiday. Every year on that day, Mao and other top officials of the Communist Party would step onto Tiananmen Gate to be worshiped by hundreds of thousands of people in Tiananmen Square. Many Chinese people's dream would become a reality that day; they would see their highest ruler, whom they called "the red sun in our hearts." Organized masses would sing and dance, expressing their loyalty and gratitude toward Mao and other party officials, including the vice-chairman of the party and Mao's "close comrade," Lin Biao.

But it was different in 1971. The celebration at Tiananmen Square was canceled. More shocking events followed.

On a late October day, regular classes were canceled. Our elementary school head spent the whole day reading government documents to us through loudspeakers installed in every classroom. I couldn't believe my ears. The documents accused Lin Biao, Mao's second-in-command and his institutional successor, of attempting to kill Mao. Allegedly, on September 13, after a failed military coup,

Lin Biao, his wife, his son, and a few followers had tried to escape China. When their plane had crashed on the way to the Soviet Union, everyone in it had died. Now, I understood why the October 1 celebration on Tiananmen Square had been canceled.

I felt short of breath. I couldn't imagine anything more astounding than this. The school head's voice was clear and firm. However, I felt as if I were in a dream. Just yesterday, we'd lined up under Mao's portrait as we did every morning. Not only had we bid Mao live forever, but we'd also wished Lin Biao good health by chanting, "May Vice-Chairman Lin be healthy and forever healthy."

I held my breath and listened. I couldn't get used to the fact that the documents called Lin Biao by his name instead of calling him Vice-Chairman Lin as we always did.

During the Cultural Revolution, it was the norm for a person to be labeled and treated as a class enemy, but Lin Biao wasn't just any individual. He represented Mao. He was Mao's helper in launching the Cultural Revolution. If Mao was our god, Lin Biao was his prophet. In a way, Mao was a holy figure for the ordinary people, and Lin Biao was still a human. He was below Mao but above everyone else.

Why did every one of Mao's closest comrades, first Liu Shaoqi, chairman of China, and now Lin Biao, turn out to be his enemies? Why was our great leader Chairman Mao, who was loved by all Chinese people, hated by the people who knew him the best? These were the obvious questions that should have come to everyone's mind. However, I had no time to figure things out for myself. The government decided for us that we *must* hate Lin Biao. Derogatory and spiteful words gushed out from the loudspeaker, calling Lin Biao "a bourgeois egomaniac, a conspirator, a two-faced counter-revolutionary, a traitor, a representative of the landlord, rich farmer, counter-revolutionary, bad element, and rightist within the country, as well as a representative of the foreign imperialist, revisionist, and counter-revolutionary."

Somehow, I wasn't as angry as I should have been when I heard that there had been a plot to kill Mao, the person we were supposed to love. Every day, we wished him longevity and expressed our feelings for him in songs like this one:

> *The sky is big, the earth is big,*
> *But the party's kindness is bigger.*
> *Father is close, Mother is close,*
> *But Chairman Mao is closer.*

Logically, when someone plans to assassinate the person we love, we should be outraged, but I wasn't.

There could be only one explanation: I never loved Mao, though I thought I did and tried to prove it. Love is a natural emotion, not an obligation. Our love for Mao was a requirement and a precondition to avoiding prison or persecution.

For days, we listened to the head of the school read a secret document allegedly written by Lin Biao's son and the son's accomplices. The title was *Project 571 Summary*. It was a plan to overthrow Mao by force. I was awed by the means proposed to kill Mao, including using a flamethrower.

The summary called Mao "the largest feudal tyrant in Chinese history" and described China as a nation where peasants didn't have enough clothing and food. It criticized the Youth Sent-Down Movement as a "disguised punishment of reform through labor." It also pointed out that the national economy had been stagnant for more than 10 years.

Up to this point, I had attended numerous rallies against counter-revolutionaries, but this was the first time that I was told what the class enemies had said. Surprisingly, I agreed with many things in the summary. The grim picture of China it painted was the China that I lived in, only I hadn't been able to articulate it before. I used to suspect that the people's suffering that I saw was random and regional and was not the party's intention; instead, it was caused by individuals who didn't implement party policies correctly. From the summary, however, I knew that the suffering was a nationwide phenomenon. I felt somewhat relieved and encouraged because someone else also saw that the emperor had no clothes.

The event changed me in a subtle yet profound way.

My view of Mao and his Cultural Revolution didn't change overnight. Mao was still my god, but the halo above his head had dimmed somewhat. I came to realize that Mao could be questioned. He wasn't invincible. He wasn't the bright red sun that everyone worshiped. Some people dared to challenge his authority and even wanted him dead. Of course, in public, we still praised him every day.

Not long after the nationwide campaign to denounce Lin Biao started, a few men from Factory 221 came to Beijing and visited Mother at the chemistry department. Though they wore military uniforms, they were not the ones who had come last time with the news of Father's death. This time, the military men told Mother that Father hadn't died from an illness, but from Lin Biao and his followers' persecution. They said that gaining power in the Chinese nuclear weapons program had been a major part of Lin Biao's plan to overthrow Mao and that Factory 221 had been a "heavily hit disaster area." Mother was told that Father had died during interrogations because he'd refused to admit his "crimes." He had been accused of being a Kuomintang secret agent and of having his students and colleagues sabotage the nuclear weapons program. He'd rejected the false accusations and refused to implicate his students and colleagues.

Listening to Mother relaying what the military men had said, I couldn't control my tears. Although Mother and I had already guessed that Father's death was due to persecution, hearing that a loved one had died in such a horrific manner was still the worst thing that could happen to any family.

When Mother talked to me, she didn't cry. She bit her lip and looked out the window. The fire of anger was burning in her eyes like two little torches.

"If Lin Biao hadn't died," Mother said, "they would still

be lying to us."

"Who did it?" I asked her, wiping tears off my face.

"I asked the military men the same question. 'Who were those people? Where are they now?'" She turned her gaze from the window and looked at me.

According to Mother, one military man said, "The whole thing in Factory 221 was Lin Biao's doing, just like in the rest of the country. Your husband was a victim of the class struggle of two lines: Chairman Mao's proletarian revolutionary line and Lin Biao's counter-revolutionary line. Where there is a struggle, there are victims. Your husband happened to be one of the victims. The heads of the military workgroup in Factory 221 were Lin Biao's followers and are now being interrogated. Justice is being served for your husband."

Mother said to the military man, "My husband was killed. It was a murder. The leaders need to take responsibility, and so do the murderers who killed my husband. They also need to be brought to justice."

"The masses were used by the Lin Biao counter-revolutionary clique," the military man said. "They were just following orders and, therefore, cannot be punished."

It rained the whole day off and on. We watched as a few men took a wooden crate four feet long, three feet wide, and three feet high off a vehicle, into our apartment building, and into our home. It had all Father's belongings in it. Somehow, the few leather suitcases that Father had taken with him had all disappeared, and all he had left was this rough wooden crate. On the face of the crate was Father's name written in black ink. It was in Father's beautiful handwriting.

The men put the crate on the concrete floor of Mother's room and took off.

Father was finally home after 11 long years. Now he was with the people who loved him dearly. Here he could rest his battered body and nurture his tired soul. *He cannot be hurt anymore, not by anybody and not by anything,* I thought. Tears mixed with the rain and ran down my face. It didn't dry for a long time.

Mother sent me away before she opened the crate. She wanted to be alone with Father one last time. She didn't want me to see what was in the crate.

After Lin Biao's death, Father's colleagues were released from the prisons. Many of them were his students from the university. They were the ones who'd gathered his belongings and put them in the crate. A student and colleague of Father's warned Mother that they had found evidence on Father's clothing that he had been tortured. To preserve the evidence, they hadn't washed the clothes.

But Mother told me that the crate was almost empty: no books, no notebooks, and no letters that our family had written to him. Big Brother said that Father had a Go game (a Chinese chess game) made of animal bones. It was Father's family heirloom, and he would bring it home on his vacations and play it with Big Brother. The Go game was not in the wooden crate. All Mother saw was one outfit of Father's with mud on it. Father's student told us that Father had died in the spring and it had been raining. He might have fallen in the rain. I was surprised that there were no bloody clothes.

❧

Some of the people from Factory 221, who were released from the prisons after Lin Biao's death, had a gathering in Beijing in honor of Father. I wanted to go to the meeting; however, Mother wouldn't let me.

"You are too young," she said.

She went alone, taking a notebook with her.

According to Mother, the mood of the meeting was somber, and people were weeping. The nation's best and brightest gathered together to mourn one of their own, the one who didn't make it home.

Immediately after she came back from the meeting, I took out Mother's notebook from her bag and read it. In their own words, the former colleagues described Father as the person we knew: honest, kind, and a man of integrity. According to the people in the gathering, Father was so thoughtful that he often bought meals before the cafeteria closed for his colleagues who overslept or worked late. As the director of the division, he often took on the dangerous task of handling explosives himself. At the same time, he was so humble that when he was asked to sit in the center when the photo of the division was taken, he rejected the idea and insisted on sitting toward the end.

When I read Father's story, I remembered a conversation with my uncle, Father's big brother. Uncle had told me shortly after Father's passing, "Your father never looked down upon anyone, and he truly believed other people were as good as he was and as intelligent as he was." I knew Uncle had been telling the truth. Father was humble and thoughtful.

Once, when I was walking with Father on campus during one of his trips to Beijing, a former colleague of his rode a bicycle toward us and recognized him. When the man was about to jump off the bicycle to greet him, Father smiled and said, "Please don't stop for me." I had never seen anyone act in this way before or after. In Father, I saw a modest, elegant, and sincere man, the kind of person who was already rare after the communists took over China and who became extinct after the Cultural Revolution.

As I was going through Mother's notes, I understood why Mother didn't want me to attend the meeting. Father's colleagues had painted a gruesome picture of Factory 221.

The Cultural Revolution at Factory 221 lagged behind the national movement by at least a year. While school classes were suspended, universities were banned from accepting new students, and factories were reducing productivity so people could focus on the witch hunt, the government sheltered Factory 221 from the Cultural Revolution till 1967 so that the people there could make a hydrogen bomb. To

Mao, China didn't need college students, and the people didn't need life necessities, but he had to have his nuclear weapons.

When the Cultural Revolution finally hit Factory 221, two opposing mass organizations were formed and fought each other to prove that they were the real Mao loyalists and that the others were fake. All research and production halted. The services of shuttle buses between the living quarters and the research areas stopped. The people who had made the nuclear bombs used the most primitive weapons to fight each other: spears, bricks, and Tibetan-style slingshots. Young people stood on top of the buildings behind makeshift bunkers constructed of rocks and bricks. With hard hats on, they scoped out "enemy" activities in the distance with binoculars.

Factory 221 was in utter chaos, which was a great concern for the government. To ensure the nuclear weapons program continued without interference, Mao, the butcher who'd slaughtered his way into power, mobilized the Chinese military, the most efficient killing machine in the world against the country's own civilians. In 1967, Mao, Chinese Premier Zhou Enlai, and other Chinese leaders sent 22 telegrams ordering martial law to be enforced in nuclear-weapons-related research institutes, plants, and test bases. Factory 221 was one of them. "The Cultural Revolution can only be carried out in spare time," the telegrams dictated. From then on, Father's life and his colleagues' lives were in the hands of the Chinese military.

Poisoned by class hatred instilled by the communist

government, the military saw the people at Factory 221, especially the educated ones, as enemies and used the most barbaric means—bats, furniture, or even hot plates—to torture them. They forced the victims to stand close to a fire and singed them; sometimes they bent the victims' fingers upward to inflict pain and called the punishment "mini tiger bench." The military men didn't hesitate to kick women or hit them with bats. They were not afraid to kill people because they were told by the leaders of the military workgroup, "If we don't kill people, the situation will not change."

Father was arrested in March 1970 when people were forced to gather in a big yard by the military men, who were armed with rifles. On the stage, a military officer announced that Father was a class enemy and ordered his arrest. He was separated from other prisoners, but the people in the meetings said they had seen him limping and moving with difficulty. Father was tortured.

I was shaking when I read the scenes described by Father's colleagues. I couldn't imagine what Father, a kind and gentle man, had been forced to go through.

From Father's colleagues, I learned how cruel the communists were. Before this, I hadn't known that the "most lovable people," the Chinese military, were animal-like. I didn't know that the term "human" was falsely inclusive. The military men deliberately and systematically tortured their fellow human beings. The thought made the hair on the back of my neck stand up.

I cried as I read the notes. Each time I turned the page, I was afraid that I would read something even more unbearable. If the Lin Biao event had put doubts in my mind about Mao and his regime, Mother's notes sent me on a path to search for the real cause of people's suffering.

It would be a long road. At this point, due to a lack of information and courage, I failed to admit that Mao, our highest leader, a symbol of China, the source of the Chinese people's pride, and a big part of our self-identity, was evil. I accepted what I was told: Father's death was Lin Biao and his followers' doing.

CHAPTER SEVEN

1972

In spring, I graduated from elementary school and entered junior high school. The school, founded and built by American missionaries in 1916, sat high above the street and was surrounded by a five-foot-high brick wall. An athletic field lay on the north side of the campus, and an auditorium stood on the south. The red walls of the two-story brick buildings peeked through from behind the pine trees' dark green crowns. The long history and the good reputation of the school attracted good teachers. However, in 1966, the red storm of the Cultural Revolution swept through the school. We were told that teachers had been abused by the Red Guards. Some of the teachers had been tied to trees and beaten by their students.

At home, I didn't talk about Father. Some wounds could be healed by tending them; some had to be left alone. After

Father's death, I was like someone stuck on a cliff; looking up, I might survive, but looking down, I would fall. To go on with my life, I tried to avoid thinking about Father and his death. Mother was the only one who would bring up the subject of Father. It often happened after she heard rumors about him.

One day, immediately after Mother came home from work and even before she put down her bag, she told me, "Today I heard that Premier Zhou was so infuriated when he heard of your father's death that he smashed his mug." I could see the glow in her eyes. She was like a dehydrated person, stranded in the desert, seeing a mirage.

"The premier was upset because your father was among the very few experts who didn't study abroad," Mother said. "The premier said, 'He was educated in China. He was our own expert.'" Mother lifted her head, and her eyes were bright with pride.

On another day, Mother said that she had heard that when Japanese Prime Minister Kakuei Tanaka had visited China in 1972, he'd asked about Father.

"The Japanese prime minister may not have known your father's name," Mother said, "but he heard there was an explosives expert who came up with the formula for the high explosives that detonated the bomb. That expert was your father." Mother was proud.

None of this mattered to me anymore. Father's death had changed my world. When he had been alive, he'd been my role model. I'd always wanted to grow up to be like him: a good person who did important things for China.

I'd thought that being honest and hardworking would be rewarded. I had tried hard to follow orders and be the best at everything I did, just like Father. But now he was dead. His death had taken away a sense of security. The world had become a hostile place, and life was a treacherous course filled with tragedies.

Gradually, the rumors about Father stopped. Even Mother rarely mentioned him, but we all knew that everyone in our family had an open wound in their heart.

Lily was the first friend in school with whom I talked about Father. That week, the school sent our class to help a troop stationed nearby build an athletic field. It was one of the "supporting the military projects." One day, during a break, Lily and I found shade under a big tree. We lay on the ground, put our hands under our heads, and looked up. The high-noon sun filtered through the thick crown of the tree and sprinkled bright dots on Lily's youthful face. She cried when I talked about Father.

The second and last friend with whom I spoke about Father was Dong. A female student cadre with a deep voice, she had a high level of "class consciousness." Her older sister was a sent-down youth, and every month, Dong sent the sister the government-mouthpiece *Red Flag* magazine for her to read. When I told Dong about Father, she said in an authoritarian manner, "If a mother dies, that's a real loss for the family, but when a father dies, the biggest loss is to the household income." I was so shocked that I was speechless. I didn't know some people felt this way about their fathers. I stopped talking to my friends about Father after that.

Unlike in elementary school, where our time was consumed with the Cultural Revolution—rallies, meetings, and protests—in junior high school, the number of mass rallies was reduced, and the time we spent in the classroom increased. It was said that the Lin Biao event had affected Mao physically and mentally, and that could have been the reason the ordinary people had a brief break from the endless witch hunt. Another reason that we were allowed to have some peaceful time in school was that Mao's loyalists were busy cleaning out Lin Biao's followers within the government and the military.

For more than a year, our academic study was almost uninterrupted by the political movement. The teachers were so enthusiastic about teaching that they acted as if they had forgotten the suffering they'd endured at the hands of their former students. Best of all, we had real textbooks. In elementary school, we didn't have textbooks for Chinese reading and writing classes. To teach us, Teacher Li copied the articles from the party-controlled newspapers on the blackboard, and we copied them down in our notebooks. She then selected new characters from the articles to teach us.

I remember how excited I was when I received the brand-new textbooks at the beginning of the first semester in junior high school. We only spent half a day in school. After lunch, I sat in our apartment at our dining table and made covers for all my textbooks with pages from magazines. I then spent the whole afternoon reading the Chinese literature textbook out loud from cover to cover. I grabbed the book tightly with both hands as if it were my best friend. My throat hurt, but I didn't mind.

I excelled at academic studies and was appointed one of the five student cadres in my class. My responsibility was to collect homework for the teachers and organize the half-hour English practice in the mornings. I participated in school activities and joined the honor-student type of groups.

The situation in our family improved somewhat, also. The Second Ministry of Machinery Industry brought my brothers back from the countryside and arranged for them to be trained in Beijing so that they could work in the factories of the ministry. The arrangement was considered compensation for my family's loss due to Father's death.

CHAPTER EIGHT

1973

By fall, the university where Mother worked started accepting new students, and she was allowed to teach again, although no one in her department told her that she wasn't a class enemy anymore.

"Allowing me to teach implied that they admitted they were wrong," Mother said when I asked her if anyone had apologized for persecuting her. Things in China were always implied; nothing was spelled out with words. People in power would never admit their wrongdoing. Mother was happy that she could teach again and was willing to move on.

The morning of the first day of teaching, she put on a light gray button-down shirt and a pair of trousers of matching color. Her shoulder-length hair was held back with two black hairpins behind her ears, making it neat and smooth. In her right hand was her black tote bag, and in her left arm, she held a stack of notes and handouts that she had prepared for the class. When I opened our apartment door for her, my heart beat fast. I couldn't tell if it was because I hadn't seen her so happy for a long time or because I was nervous for her because she hadn't been teaching for seven years. Mother smiled and walked out the door with her chin up and shoulders back. She had a spring in her step.

When Mother came home in the evening, she looked tired. A strand of hair had escaped the hairpin, and the spark in her eyes was gone.

"Don't tell anyone, because no one would believe you," she said. "Today, in my class, one of my students insisted that five plus five is five." She shook her head.

The new students were not ready for college courses. Mao had condemned the practice of having college entrance exams as a part of a "revisionist educational line," and because of that, the new students were not selected based on entrance exams. They were called "worker-peasant-soldier students." They became university students because their peers and superiors recommended them based on their political standing and work performance instead of academic merit. Most of the students hadn't finished high school, and some hadn't even finished elementary school.

The math department was overwhelmed because they had to teach the new students junior high school math and high school math.

My neighbor Aunt Gao, who was a math teacher, solicited help from me. "Help me correct my students' homework," she said. I was thrilled that I, a 15-year-old junior high school student, had been given such an important task. I felt my time in school had not been wasted.

❧

My cherished opportunity to learn in a quiet environment was destroyed at the end of my second year in junior high school when the government started another political movement within school systems, this one targeting teachers. Rebellious students smashed windows and broke furniture in schools. At the urging of our school officials, big-character posters denouncing teachers were put up all over the campus. The government encouraged the students throughout the country to "grow horns on the heads and thorns on the bodies" in fighting against a "resurgence of revisionist lines of education." Students who didn't rise against the teachers were called "revisionists' little lambs."

Our classroom was chaotic every day.

When Kai woke up from his nap in the middle of a chemistry class and hopped onto his desk, I sensed trouble. Not long ago, the boy with round black eyes and thick eyebrows, who was a head taller than most of our classmates, had sprayed everyone in my class with a fire extinguisher. He'd laughed as we'd cleaned white foam off our hair and clothes.

Now, in chemistry class, Kai stood on his desk, laughing. He tucked his hands into the pockets of his dark cotton-padded jacket to keep them warm. The room was cold because the windows were broken, a casualty of some students' revolutionary actions in the new political movement. We had no radiators in the classroom. To keep us warm, a worker would start a coal-burning stove in the middle of the room every morning, but some boys would put it out as soon as they came to school. They wanted to create an excuse to leave school early.

The chemistry teacher rushed over to urge Kai to come down from his desk. The woman, who was in her late thirties with short hair and wire-rimmed glasses, extended her hand to the student. In an environment where teachers had become the main targets of the political movement, most didn't dare discipline the students. They would just leave the classroom when the students became too unruly. The chemistry teacher was an exception.

Kai refused to get off the desk; instead, he jumped to the next desk and then another, all the way to the back of the classroom. There he threw his head back and laughed. Behind Kai was the back wall, which had been white until he and a few boys had thrown coal on it out of boredom one day. Now the wall was black and white, like a chaotic painting.

When the teacher walked toward Kai, he jumped off the desk, picked up a dustpan from the corner of the room, and took off. A few minutes later, he returned through the front door with a dustpan full of dirt. Standing in front of the class, next to the teacher, he had a wide grin on his face. It looked as if he planned to toss the dirt on the students, so they started to panic. Some tried to hide under the desk, and some went for the back door. Trying to stop Kai, the chemistry teacher grabbed the dustpan, but he wouldn't let go. During the struggle, he lifted the dustpan above the teacher's head and dumped it on her. The dirt covered her from head to toe. Watching her run out of the classroom, he laughed, still holding the empty dustpan.

I couldn't believe what I had just seen. It was normal for Kai to disturb the class and harass other students, but this was the first time he had done anything violent to a teacher.

For the first time in my life, I dared to admit to myself that I didn't like the government's policy—not just the way some individuals carried it out, but the policy itself. It was the new movement that allowed bullies like Kai to abuse a teacher. Under the communist rules, being educated was bourgeois. Ignorance was glorified, and being rude was being revolutionary. During the Cultural Revolution, many people prided themselves on being a "big old rough (Da Lao Cu)."

A few girls from our class went to see the chemistry teacher in her office later that day. She sat behind her desk and had already cleaned up, but I could see her eyes were red and puffy behind her glasses. The students settled around the desk, some sitting in chairs and some standing. I stood across the desk from the teacher.

"I have just told the school officials that I will not be teaching your class anymore," the teacher said. My heart sank. We had lost a good teacher. I felt abandoned, but at the same time, I didn't want her to stay and suffer, either.

"What can we do?" a girl sitting next to the teacher

asked her. "We are tired of Kai's behavior."

"You cannot count on the school to do anything," the teacher said.

I nodded, agreeing with her. The student cadres in the class had complained to the school officials many times, and finally, the officials had talked to Kai's parents, which had upset him a great deal. The next day, he'd threatened the student cadres in class: "I will crack your head open like a watermelon with a brick." His intense eyes were open wide under his thick dark eyebrows, and a big black mole on his left cheek moved up and down as his mouth opened and closed.

"There is not much a teacher can do because we will be accused of suppressing the students," the chemistry teacher said, leaning back in her chair. She looked at each student's face as she did in class, only now her eyes were filled with disappointment and helplessness.

The chemistry teacher never taught us again. Her replacement was a young male teacher whose nickname was Lao Mian, meaning "Old Mellow." Lao Mian didn't seem to care about anything or be bothered by anything. He rarely managed to finish any experiment in class. Each time he tried to heat chemicals in a beaker on an alcohol burner, the boy who sat in the first row would fan the flames away from the beaker. As a result, the chemical reaction never took place because the chemicals never reached the desired temperature.

Time was wasted in chaos, and I finished junior high school in disappointment.

CHAPTER NINE

1975

After winter break, half of the approximately 300 junior high school graduates in our school went to the countryside to work as farmhands, and the other half stayed on to go to high school. Unlike a few years earlier when my brothers had been sent away to border areas and had been expected to take root there, the government now sent junior high school and high school graduates to nearby counties to do farm work, and after two years, the youths were expected to return to Beijing and work in factories.

I decided to go to high school, not only to postpone the two years that I had to "serve" in the countryside but also to spend more time in school. With most known student bullies choosing to go to the countryside, I expected that high school would be a place to learn instead of a place for unruly students to torment teachers and fellow students.

I started to fantasize about the quiet classrooms and the calm teachers.

Reality rarely matches fantasy, however. Within days of entering high school, I was on a northbound bus out of the city with my classmates. Our school had sent my class of 30 students to dig a fishpond for a people's commune and to be re-educated by the peasants.

A bundle made of a quilt and a few pieces of clothing rested on my lap, and a washbasin sat underneath my seat. Inside my pocket were a few food ration coupons and some money that I'd gotten from Mother.

About 40 minutes later, the red and yellow bus turned off the tree-lined city street and continued on a country road. The bus bounced over the holes and ditches while we jostled around in our seats as if we were drunk. When the bus finally stopped, we found ourselves surrounded by vast farmland, dry and barren. We got off the bus and walked toward a cluster of about a dozen small houses. The wind was strong, blowing our hair and fluttering our clothes. I later learned that the place had the nickname "Big Wind Mouth" because of its year-round high wind.

A narrow room with a dirt floor was the temporary home for the 15 female students. The only bed stretched from wall to wall. It was made of a few boards supported by a single layer of bricks. A layer of hay covered the boards. We put our sheets and quilts on the hay and slept on it at night. There was no stove in the room. We slept with our sweaters on and put winter jackets on top of the quilts to keep ourselves warm.

Five students were selected to be our cooks. They collected the food ration coupons and money that we'd brought from home. The cooks bought food and cooked for the whole class. We each had bok choy soup, two steamed buns made with flour, and two made with cornmeal every meal. There was no meat because, unlike for rice or flour, there were no ration coupons for meat. To buy rice noodles, eggs, starch, pork, and so on, every family was given a ration book. The families couldn't give their only ration book to the students.

Every day, we worked hard on the fishpond. The girls dug the dirt with picks and shovels and put it in wheelbarrows. The boys pushed the dirt away. We were not the first ones to dig the pond. When we started, the pond was already deeper than a grown man, and dirt was piled up around it. A few long and narrow boards bridged the berm and the level ground so that more dirt could be taken away with the wheelbarrows. With a heavy load and only one wheel, the wheelbarrows were difficult to control. The boys struggled to balance them. Their heavy breathing could be heard from far away. For some reason, the deeper we dug, the wetter the dirt became. Eventually, dirt became mud. It stuck to the shovels. Someone said that because it was early spring, the ground had started to thaw and that was where the water was coming from.

We didn't complain. We didn't want to be seen as bourgeois. We wanted to be proletarian, like the peasants who were supposed to re-educate us, although we'd had no contact with them except the one time a peasant cadre had come to our room after dinner to read editorials from the newspapers to us.

We left Big Wind Mouth after five weeks without finishing the fishpond. The next class would continue digging. Now, looking back, I suspect that the goal was never to finish the "fishpond." The peasants were never present to monitor our work or to tell us how big and how deep it should be. The school just wanted to send the students to the countryside to endure hardship so that we could be made into "successors of the proletarian revolutionary missions."

For almost half of our time in high school, the school officials sent us to do physical labor to help us get rid of bourgeois thoughts and transform our worldview to that of the proletarian. After the fishpond, the school made us take bricks out of a brick kiln as big as a building for a people's commune. We helped peasants harvest wheat and vegetables in the field. We also helped stores sell vegetables.

For a whole semester, the school wanted us to "learn from the factory workers" by sending us to a trucking maintenance workshop for a transportation company. The state-owned company had many trucks. Every four years, each truck was taken apart for thorough cleaning and maintenance.

Although working in the workshop would take away my time to learn in school, I saw it as an opportunity to restore my faith in Mao. I had been having doubts about political movements in which millions of people suffered, and the mere thought of questioning the correctness of Mao and his party scared me. In a nation where everyone professed his loyalty to Mao and the party, I didn't want to alienate myself. Not only was I afraid of being persecuted, but I was also afraid of not being on the right side. The communists claimed the moral high ground and said all the right things: equality, serving the people, and representing the majority's interests. Questioning the government meant rejecting these values. We often defend an ideology that we believe in, no matter how flawed or deadly it is, only because it sounds right and because we identify with it. I couldn't give up my identity as a good person.

Like the soldiers, the factory workers were given high social status in Mao's China. Mao praised them as "the most far-sighted, the most selfless, and the most thoroughly revolutionary" and said that they "must exercise leadership in everything." The people with whom I was familiar were educated—teachers in my high school or the university where I lived. They were targets of the political movement and had a deep sense of grievance against it, although they didn't express their feelings publicly. I expected to see a different attitude toward the Cultural Revolution from the workers. I needed to know that Mao was right and that the workers supported him. I saw my own view as being dangerous and wanted to correct it because I didn't want to "stand on the opposite side of the people," as *People's Daily* often warned.

With the task I had given to myself, I headed to the workshop.

My job was cleaning pistons. In a big room with a tall ceiling and large windows, I squatted on the concrete floor by a metal workbench, hovering over a washbasin filled with diesel and scrubbing the pistons with a piece of sandpaper. From time to time, I lifted my head to watch the workers, expecting to see the enthusiastic, outgoing, generous, and helpful people that the government propaganda machine had portrayed.

The workers didn't seem to be eager to re-educate us. The first day went by, and I didn't hear uplifting speeches or encouraging words. I didn't see any worker who matched the image in my head, either. The movies, plays, and posters at the time depicted workers as people of immense power. As a popular saying put it, "When the workers roar, the earth shakes three times." In my imagination, a typical worker was short and stocky, with his sleeves rolled up above his elbows, showing chiseled forearms. The workers I saw were ordinary. In their greasy blue work shirts, some workers worked hard, and some dragged their feet. Some joked around, and others kept to themselves. They were just people, like the teachers.

After work was political study time. I sat on a wooden bench by the window, waiting to hear the workers' speeches. At school, during political study sessions, everyone had to give speeches showing their support for the government. "Speaking well or not is a matter of skill; speaking or not is a matter of your attitude," a teacher had told us. *The political study session will be the time to witness the workers' class consciousness,* I told myself.

There was a wooden table in the middle of the room. The newspapers with the communist indoctrination articles covered the table like a tablecloth. On one side of the table, sitting in a chair, was the manager, a man in his forties. Opposite him were three older men sitting on a wooden bench in their greasy dark blue worker's uniforms.

I later learned that the three men were the former owners of three automobile maintenance shops. In the early 1950s, the communist government had confiscated their businesses and made them into the state-owned trucking maintenance workshop that I was working for now. The three former owners were made to work as workers in the new workshop. They had been labeled class enemies because they'd exploited workers by employing them before the communists took over their workshops. The three ex-owners were under the revolutionaries' watchful eye. They had to "obey and behave and not speak up or act the way they want." During each political study session, they had to sit where everyone could see them. If anyone accused them of avoiding political study and resisting thought reform, the consequences would be unimaginable.

Workers from other groups started to come. Instead of sitting on the metal stools and wooden benches scattered around the workbenches, they sat on the concrete floor, with their backs against the walls.

Feeling awkward sitting up high, I joined the other workers on the floor. Now the only people who weren't sitting on the floor were the four men at the wooden table covered by the newspapers. I was curious to see how the workers were going to give speeches from behind the legs of the workbenches.

The political study session lasted 30 minutes, and no one said a word. It didn't seem the workers cared about the political study at all. Some had their legs stretched out and their eyes closed. Others were cleaning their greasy hands with cloths. When the bell rang at the end of the session, everyone, including the ones who had dozed off, sprang up from the floor and left the room in a hurry without a word.

It was the same the next day, and the third. A few days had passed, and I didn't know what the manager or anyone in the meeting sounded like. The manager didn't even bother to read the newspaper or have someone else read it to us.

I was fascinated by the workers. Under the communists, we lost our right to remain silent. At school, silence during political studies was not allowed because it was deemed a sign of resentment and resistance against the party. Some teachers would reveal their true thoughts privately, but in public, they always praised the party. If a teacher didn't want to say anything in class or in a meeting against his will, he would read an article from the newspaper to us or have someone else read it to avoid complete silence.

The workers were not afraid. They were proletarians, which put them on the "right" side and made them less fearful than the teachers. Since they were already doing physical labor and receiving low wages, the workers didn't have much downward mobility if they did get punished.

The workers' behavior made me so happy that I was

laughing inside. I realized that I was not the only one who was resentful toward the Cultural Revolution and fed up with the endless political study sessions used to "unify thoughts." I was not a bad person.

My experience at the workshop told me that not only were my family, my neighbors, and my teachers fed up with the Cultural Revolution, but even the workers were extremely resentful of it. They'd gained nothing but a 30-minute political study session after eight hours of work. After so many years, only Mao and his closest allies supported the Cultural Revolution.

However, I couldn't see any sign of the end of the misery. No matter how angry people are, anger doesn't topple a dictatorship. Actions do. There is a gap between recognizing evil and acting against it. The gap is fear, and the bridge is courage. Some gaps will never be crossed, and the result is thousands of years of dictatorship. The silent majority's anger toward the Cultural Revolution never turned into meaningful action.

I thought the Cultural Revolution would never end.

CHAPTER TEN

1976

The Cultural Revolution entered its tenth year. It started when I was eight, and now I was 18, in my last year in high school. By now, my brothers had finished training and were working as factory workers. Big Brother worked in another part of the country, while Second Brother stayed in Beijing.

In March, a rain of meteorites hit northeastern China. Three big rocks penetrated five feet of frozen earth and came to rest at a depth of 21 feet in the ground.

The Chinese believed that each star in the sky represented a person on Earth. When a shooting star flew across the sky, it was said that a person had just passed. Three big rocks from the sky indicated the death of three high-ranking officials. Premier Zhou Enlai had died in January that year; people wondered who would be the next.

In July, Zhu De, commander-in-chief of the People's Liberation Army, died.

There were three fallen rocks in the ground, and two of China's highest-ranking leaders were dead. Who would be the third? The answer seemed to be obvious, but no one dared to say it.

September 9, 1976, was like any other day. After school, a friend and I picked up shards of broken glass from the streets near the school, put them in a white bucket, and took them to a recycling station to make money for class activities. We walked into a yard enclosed by a chain-link fence. Piles of scrap metal and stacks of newspapers and old books were everywhere in the yard. A shed with a rusty corrugated metal roof sat in the middle of the yard. A man was locking up the place.

"It is awfully early to close up," I said, looking up at the sky. It was the middle of the afternoon; the sun was still high.

"My boss told me to lock up the station right now and go home to wait for important news," the man said, avoiding looking at us.

My friend and I looked at each other. Without saying a word, we understood what had happened: Mao was dead.

We went back to school and sat in the classroom. More students came and joined us. They must have heard about the important news, too. Before long, we heard it over the loudspeaker above the blackboard. In great contrast to the aggressive manner of the radio announcers those days, a male announcer used a somber voice and read the news extremely slowly. He paused between words. Before he finished his first sentence, we knew Mao was dead.

I remember that I wasn't very sad, but I knew Mao's death was a major event. I was concerned. Things had been horrible for years. The popular belief at the time was that the people's misery was not Mao's fault; instead, it was the fault of the people around him, particularly his wife, Jiang Qing, who was the deputy director of the Central Cultural Revolution Small Group, the organization that was under Mao's control and in charge of the nationwide purge. I feared that after Mao's death, his wife would be even more out of control and the situation in China would be even worse.

On hearing the news, the students in my class sprang into action. During the 10 years of the Cultural Revolution, we had learned that personal feelings were more than private emotions; they were for public display. Showing the wrong emotions or even not showing enough right emotions could be a reason for persecution. Before we even had the time to examine our feelings, we needed to act the way we were expected. Like bees whose nest was on fire, we got busy. We took money out of our class's piggy bank and collected donations from everyone who had a few cents in their pockets. We bought thin wire and white paper. The school gave us some black fabric. We made small white paper flowers to pin on our shirts and black armbands for everyone to wear. We made a wreath.

I participated in all activities.

I still believed that it was Lin Biao, not Mao, who had caused Father's death. Although things happened every day that made me question Mao and his party, much stronger voices came from every direction—school, media, and other people—telling me how great Mao was. Obvious things would take years to become clear to me. I couldn't imagine that our great leader and the Chinese people's savior was evil.

The next morning, we sat in the classroom, waiting for the newspapers to come. There would be important articles in them by the government telling us what to do after Mao's death.

The classroom was quiet. The door was open, and we could feel the pleasant breeze of late summer. A girl started crying from the classroom next door. It started out low but grew louder. Eventually it became all-out howling. She was mourning the death of Mao. In the days after Mao's death, a crying Chinese was considered a good Chinese. Soon another class joined in, and then a third. It was contagious. The sound of crying came from every direction, like a competition.

Our classroom was quiet until Dong, the girl who had told me that the loss of a father only meant reduced income for the family, started crying. Like a dam breaking and the water bursting forth, she cried hard and long. She shuddered, and at times, she couldn't catch her breath. I was amazed by her emotional outpouring and couldn't help but wonder if she would cry this hard if her own father passed away. By the time the newspapers came, she had put her head on the desk, dozing off.

That night, six students, including me, guarded the shrine in the auditorium hall. We discussed why the shrine needed to be guarded. Would someone be stealing the wreaths? Would the class enemies set the shrine on fire? We didn't know. What we knew was that because Mao had died, we needed to do as much as possible to express our sorrow. When the night went deep, we put chairs together and slept on them.

The next morning, three friends and I went to Tiananmen Square to display our sadness publicly. We were not alone. Many people showed up in the square with white flowers on chests, black armbands on arms, and red banners or Mao's portraits in hands. Four of us held our fists next to our right ears and had our photos taken. We put on solemn-looking faces. We swore that we would fulfill Mao's wishes, whatever they were.

All the activities were not enough for me. More had to be done. A friend of mine and I decided that we wanted to see Mao's body to pay our respects.

We went to the State Council, the place Mother and I had visited more than once to try to find justice for Father, and the place where we never got to talk to anyone except the receptionists. Surprisingly, this time, after the receptionist heard our request, not only did she lift her head, not only did she look at us, but she even made a phone call. Before long, a man in a military uniform came out from the compound. My guess was that he was a low-ranking official who worked at the State Council. This was the first time that I had not been brushed off by the receptionists. Like everyone else in Beijing, the man had a white flower on his chest and a black armband on his left arm. He told us that Mao's body was not yet available for the public to view. My friend and I started crying. The official was choking up, too. He told us that there would be a public viewing in a few days. We would all have our chance to see the body, he promised. We got a little consolation from his words and walked away.

As I turned around, I saw a group of about 20 people sitting outside the State Council compound under the Chinese juniper trees. Their faces were leathered, and their clothes tattered. I realized that they had come to the capital from all over the country to seek justice, and most of them were peasants. With no independent judicial system and the party controlling everything, the peasants relied on a Chinese tradition, an archaic system dating back to imperial times in which aggrieved people who could not get justice at the local level went to the capital to implore the emperor for help, just like Mother and I had tried to do.

Unlike most people in Beijing those days, the people in front of me displayed no emotions regarding Mao's death. They had no white flowers, no black armbands, no tears, and no facial expressions. I always thought Mao was dear to the peasants because, supposedly, he was their savior. After all, without the support of the millions of Chinese peasants, Mao would not have been in power. I suspected that without radio, the peasants were not aware of Mao's death. Then I saw that the newspapers with Mao's headshot framed in black were tossed all around them. Obviously, they had been given the news.

I knew what would happen to those people: they would not be received by any officials, their pleas would not be answered, and justice would not be served. I knew this because Mother and I had experienced it. If Lin Biao had not died, the truth of Father's death would not have come out. The people outside the government compound were in an even worse situation than Mother and I were: at the end of a fruitless and frustrating day, Mother and I could go home, but these people had to seek shelter under the trees. Being peasants, coming to Beijing was a huge financial undertaking for their families. They had no money for the road and no money to stay in a hotel. Most likely, many of them had begged all the way to Beijing from their hometowns. It was September, and the weather would be getting cold soon. *Where are they going to stay?* I worried.

On the way home, I thought about what I had seen outside of the State Council compound. The poor peasants, who were supposed to love Mao the most, didn't seem to be saddened by his death at all. In my school, the harder one cried over Mao's death, the more praise one received. Some had even fainted during the nationwide funeral for Mao. Of course, not every resident in Beijing was sad about Mao's death, but most of us at least put on a performance. Those peasants didn't even pretend to be sad. I couldn't help but wonder: *When we are told by the government that everyone, especially the peasants, loves Mao, are we being lied to?*

It turned out not everybody was allowed to see Mao's corpse. I did not have a chance to see it. Nobody in our school did. I was disappointed.

Although my family and I were victims of the brutality of the party's policies, I did everything I could to display my loyalty to Mao, for loving Mao was loving China and questioning Mao made one a traitor. Years of brainwashing had taken away the ability to think independently. Mao was our god, and I didn't dare question our god.

◦

"Come here and give me a hand," Mother said, trying to pull a bed board into my room. It was an October evening, and Mao had been dead for more than a month. By now, the Gao family had moved out to their own apartment.

After Big Brother had left Beijing to work in a factory, we'd taken his bed apart and stored it in the hallway. Now Mother had the bed board up on its side and was dragging it into my room.

"What are you doing?!" I asked.

"Let's put this above your bed," Mother said. She looked determined. Her eyes were bright, as they always were when she believed she had come up with a brilliant idea.

I helped her put the thick board on the bed, not flat on top, but with one end perched on the headboard and the other end resting on two stacked pillows.

"Now, get in the bed," she ordered.

Mother wanted me to sleep underneath the "bridge."

"No," I protested.

"Listen: there will be more earthquakes coming," she said. "This is not a rumor; it is official. We had a meeting in school today. The city government told us so." Mother shook the board with her hand. It didn't move. She nodded with satisfaction. "This board will protect you if there is an earthquake tonight. The ceiling will not hit you if it falls. I would have you sleep underneath the bed if there were enough room."

About two months before, a devastating earthquake had hit Tangshan, a city less than a hundred miles away from Beijing. According to the Chinese government, 260,000 people had died in the earthquake.

The people in Beijing had felt the earthquake and were traumatized by it. On that October day, it was official: there could be more earthquakes. Second Brother and his co-workers at the factory where he worked were sent out by the government to guard a dam near Beijing. They had to sleep in the buses parked near the reservoir and wait. This was not the first time Second Brother had been called upon to guard the dam.

Mother was concerned. "What can you do if the dam does break?" she asked. "You don't even have a shovel."

For decades, the government had promoted kamikaze heroism. It had made a role model out of someone who died trying to save a couple of light poles from a river because they belonged to the country. Using one's own body as a sandbag to protect dams, only to be washed away, was also praised, which made Mother worry. Second Brother didn't know the answer to Mother's question, but he was willing to help now that he had been called upon.

After Father's death, Mother became extremely nervous about my safety. The woman who'd let me go to school alone on my first day of elementary school had changed. She treated me as if a gust of wind would take me away and never return me to her. For a while, she banned me from riding bicycles, fearing I could be killed in traffic. If I came home from school late, she would walk around the university campus, calling my name as if I were a lost kitten hiding underneath my favorite shrub. The news of more earthquakes made Mother nervous, and the makeshift shelter on my bed was the result.

"Get in there," Mother ordered.

I couldn't believe Mother had come up with such a crazy idea. We lived in a four-story building. I couldn't see how a piece of wood could hold up the building.

It was clear: either I risked being hit by the bed board during an earthquake or nobody would get any sleep that night. I decided to get in the shelter and come out when Mother went to her room.

I crawled into the shelter. The bed board was just a few inches above my face. I felt claustrophobic, and breathing became a challenge.

Not long after Mother went to her room, I heard Second Brother's rushed and excited voice. "Where is my sister? Tell her to get up."

"She is sleeping." It was Mother's voice. "Why are you home? Don't you need to protect the dam? Will there be no more earthquakes?" She kept her voice low.

"Get up! Great news!" Second Brother shouted as he burst into my room.

Mother followed.

"No more earthquakes?" I asked, crawling out from underneath the wooden board and jumping out of bed.

"Madam has been arrested," Second Brother said as he threw his hat on a desk. He tried to control himself, but his voice was quavering with excitement. His eyes were wide open. I had never seen him so emotional.

Madam was Mao's wife, Jiang Qing. When Mao died, people were afraid Jiang Qing would gain more power and throw the country deeper into hell. Now Mao's wife had been arrested a month after Mao's death, and the Cultural Revolution might really end.

It was a quiet night, and the radio was not on, but when Second Brother told us the news, I heard the music. It came from inside me. I was so happy that my heart was singing. I wanted to scream and laugh out loud. I don't think I have ever been that happy, either before or after.

"Really? Are you sure? You are not joking, are you?" Mother asked Second Brother.

"No. I am serious," he said.

"Excellent news," Mother yelled. She clapped her hands and bounced up and down without letting her feet leave the floor. She didn't want to wake up the neighbors. I joined Mother and Second Brother in celebration.

In a regime where the newspaper was the government's propaganda machine, the news was not discovered by reporters but provided to them by the authorities or leaked out to the public from insiders. The news of Jiang Qing's arrest was leaked out as a rumor before the government confirmed it. Because the rumor was so widespread, most people who heard it believed it. They celebrated it quietly and privately. Behind closed doors, many families raised their wine glasses or beer bottles, toasting the arrest of Mao's wife. Liquor was sold out in every store in Beijing, big or small. People also ate crabs to celebrate the good news; crabs symbolized bullies in China because they walked sideways. "Give me three male crabs and one female crab," a customer would order with a mysterious smile on his face, and the crab seller would return the same mysterious smile. No one needed to say it, but everyone knew that the female crab and the three male crabs symbolized Jiang Qing and her three male accomplices, who had also been arrested. They were called the Gang of Four. Some people were so overjoyed, they died of heart attacks after hearing the great news. The government confirmed the rumor soon afterward. The decision to arrest the Gang of Four had been made by the post-Mao government with support from the senior military heads. Jiang Qing and her accomplices would receive lengthy prison time.

It was a strange turn of events: a nation that had just mourned its dictator's death a month earlier was celebrating his wife's arrest. No one dared to criticize Mao, who enjoyed god-like status. All the suffering had to be someone else's doing, first Lin Biao's and now Jiang Qing's.

The Great Proletarian Cultural Revolution finally ended after 10 long, miserable years. While the post-Mao government admitted that the witch hunt had been a catastrophe, it blamed it on Mao's old age. The way the political movement ended was very telling and worrisome:

it didn't end because the people were suffering, and it didn't end because the economy was collapsing. Rather, it ended only because Mao, the slaughterer of the Chinese people, was dead. Millions of people's lives were spared.

The sad reality determined that post-Mao China would remain totalitarian. There was never an official death toll of the Cultural Revolution because the Chinese government never tallied it. People's lives were never important; they were just numbers and leverage for the communist dictators.

CHAPTER ELEVEN

1977

It happened on an October day. First, we heard it on the radio. When the newspaper came, Mother and I spread it on the dining table and read it together. Shoulder to shoulder and heads next to each other, we hovered over the newspaper for a long time. We read the news again and again. It was true: the government was allowing the college entrance exams to resume after 11 years.

"Do you know what this means?" Mother looked at me. She was smiling, and her eyes had filled with joy and hope. I nodded. I was too excited to say a word. No words were necessary; we both knew what the news meant: I might be able to go to college.

I couldn't believe how much everything had changed. The number of political movements had been greatly reduced after Mao's death. Most people who had been purged during the Cultural Revolution had been "rehabilitated" and had returned to work. Old movies were shown again, and foreigners were allowed to visit China. Now the college entrance exams were resumed.

I was already 19 and had never thought I would have a chance to go to college, even though I had grown up on a university campus. Now, if I studied hard, I might go to college, realizing the dream I'd never dared to have. It was the first time my effort would make a difference in my life. When Mao was alive, he was like a big mountain sitting on the Chinese people, and we struggled to survive the endless political movements. Only after he was dead could the Chinese people breathe easier, and millions of youths had a chance to go to college.

I wanted to go to an engineering school despite my interest in literature because writing under communists was dangerous. I buried myself in books because I had a lot of catching up to do. After all, in school, we'd spent a lot of time attending rallies or doing physical labor instead of studying academics. When I was tired from studying, I looked out of our apartment window, and through the delicate pink flowers of the Persian silk tree, I could see the corner of a white building inside the academic area of the university. I pictured myself sitting in one of the lecture halls as a university student. In my imagination, bright sunlight would shine through the big windows, and the room would be quiet, a great contrast to my junior high school classrooms. I would sit in the first row in front of the teachers because I wouldn't want to miss anything, and the teachers would stay till the bell rang because there wouldn't be student bullies to drive them out.

CHAPTER TWELVE

1978

In the peak of the summer, I took the college entrance exams. As soon as I heard that a residential sub-district office had our score sheets from the exams, I hopped on my bike. The usually short ride now seemed much longer. When I took the score sheet from an official, my hands were shaking. My scores were high enough to get into any university in the nation.

Too excited to go home, I walked to a river nearby. The 600-year-old, man-made river brought the water into the city from the Summer Palace. The water was shaded by the majestic weeping willows that lined the wide bank. I sat under the trees, where the air was cool and the ground damp. I put the score sheet on my knees and looked at the magic numbers that indicated a brand-new life for me.

The water was dark in the shade, and the long, soft

branches of the tree swayed gently in the breeze like a girl's beautiful hair. I remembered the last time I'd sat on the bank of the river. I was a first-grader and on my first field trip. That morning, we had gathered at the school, carrying food and water our parents had prepared for us. From there, we walked to the river. Teacher Li forbade the students from going in the water. We ran around on the wide banks shaded by the weeping willows. We screamed and laughed, and we played hide and seek. We had no worry in the world. Life was expected to be as smooth as the river next to us, and we were supposed to be protected like the tender moss on the bank, shielded from the sun by the trees. Not long after the field trip to the river, the Cultural Revolution had broken out, and our childhood had ended.

A dragonfly glided above the water. On the surface of the calm river, every now and then, a bubble burst, and ripples spread. The 10 years of the Cultural Revolution had taken away my childhood and my adolescence; they were gone like the water in front of me and would never return. Luckily, when I had been given an opportunity, I had taken it. I still had my youth and my future. I had hope. After all, we live in hope.

I carefully put the piece of paper in my pocket, walked out from the shadow of the weeping willow tree, and stepped into the sun.

CHAPTER THIRTEEN

1982 - 1988

In post–Cultural Revolution China, people were no longer politically overcharged. At the university I attended, academic achievement outweighed political status for most students. Soon after I entered the university, the department announced that our job assignments upon graduation would be based solely on the results of the exams. At the time, jobs were not sought but assigned. Over the next four years, I immersed myself in academic studies and excelled at them. Four years later, the department kept its promise, and I was given the job that I desired at the Chinese space program upon graduation.

On an early August day in 1982, I reported to my new job on the west side of Beijing.

The institute sat inside a big compound with walls that separated two worlds: Outside the compound was a chaotic existence filled with noise from bicycles, pedestrians, street vendors, and street sweepers. Inside the compound, it was calm and quiet, with poplar trees standing in front of gray buildings and white and lavender flowers blossoming along the wide road. I walked up to the seven-story building where the institute resided, feeling fortunate to work on something important to the nation in a peaceful environment.

The project leader of my research team was a confident, middle-aged man. He wasn't the pale, bookish type that I'd expected to see in a research institute. Instead, he was dark and had thick eyebrows and a chiseled jawline. When he spoke, he gave the impression of someone who was in charge but still personable.

"We are very happy to have you here," he said, smiling at me from behind his broad-framed glasses.

"We are working on something quite extraordinary here," he said slowly, emphasizing every word. "We will fill a void for our country when we succeed." The patriotic speech was what I wanted to hear. I sat up straight and lifted my head.

The Cultural Revolution and Father's death had made me question Mao, but they hadn't shaken my loyalty to China. Now that Mao was dead, I believed that China finally would become a normal country and people would have normal lives. The post-Mao government seemed to have changed its goal from "making sure that the nation retains its red color" to "modernizing China." Father had made his contribution to China; now it was my turn. I couldn't think of anything more meaningful than to help China develop its space industry.

"Because the project is so important," the project leader said, "no one in our group is allowed to leave his or her work to attend graduate school."

He stopped to observe my reaction. I was surprised. It seemed to be an odd time to talk about graduate school because I hadn't expressed any desire to attend one. *The leader of a small research group of 20 people seems to have a lot of power in determining people's future,* I thought. The system was set up that way. Without permission from his or her employer, no one could apply for graduate school. Though a little disappointed, I didn't allow the negative thought to dampen my enthusiasm for the new job.

In the institute, the engineers who had graduated from college before or during the Cultural Revolution were called "old graduates." Those who graduated after the Cultural Revolution were called "new graduates." That year, five new graduates, including me, joined our group.

I worked hard at my job not only because I thought it would benefit the nation, but also because being a good student or a good employee was my identity.

A few months later, I received praise from the project leader. It was winter. I had just come back from a business trip to an adjacent county. After sitting in a bumpy, cold, old bus for hours, my feet and hands were numb. With my winter jacket and a thick scarf still on, I was walking around in the office and blowing warm air on my hands when the project leader walked in, pulled up a chair, and sat down.

"Xiao Qian," he said. His eyes sparkled with the light of approval.

"Before you came," he said, "I couldn't even send a worker, let alone a college graduate, out on a cold day like this." He leaned back. Behind him was a big window with light blue window curtains pulled to the side.

I was puzzled. Taking a business trip was part of the job, and I didn't know an employee could reject a job assignment. I had heard many stories of how Father and his colleagues had endured hardships for the Chinese nuclear weapons program, and I wanted to be like them.

"You see," the project leader said, "for most people here, work means walking 10 minutes from their home to the office in the morning, sitting here for four hours, and then walking home, having lunch, and taking a nap. In the afternoon, they do the same thing. They don't want to do anything more than that." His face darkened in frustration.

Most employees, except the new graduates, lived in the apartments provided by the institute that were across the street from the office compound. During the two-hour lunch break, the employees who lived in the institute apartments could walk home to have lunch and then take a nap, while the new graduates would eat in a cafeteria and then sleep on the desks in the offices.

A project leader didn't have many means to either reward or punish his team members. Although he could stop me from getting an advanced degree, he didn't have the power to fire anyone or give anybody a bonus. China is a socialist country where, according to the government, no one should lose his or her job.

I was a little worried by the project leader's words, but I didn't allow myself to be discouraged. The success of the project would mean a lot to me. In the years after Father's death, I struggled to justify his life and his existence. In a nation where murderers walked free and the same party continued to rule, I could only find comfort in believing that Father's work had benefited the Chinese people. To contribute to the space program would be my way of honoring him.

When I found an opportunity for a free three-day seminar on subjects related to our work, I signed up. The project leader urged everyone to participate in it because it would benefit our research. The seminar was just a bus ride away, but to my surprise, only the new college graduates went. When we brought back printed materials from the seminar, we placed them on a desk for everyone to take. For two days, no one touched them.

On the third day, the news came that the institute would give employees free chickens as a bonus that afternoon. As always, the prospect of having free food energized our sleepy office. When the chickens arrived, everyone was mobilized. We laid the frozen chickens on the floor and gave each one a number. After that, each employee picked a number and found his or her chicken. It was like a sporting event. A big bird would draw a cheer, while a small chicken caused a friendly laugh or tease. The activities took a good part of the afternoon. Some excited employees wanted to go home and put their chicken in the refrigerator. The project leader waved his hand and said: "Go. Take off for the day." With a smile, the employees walked out of the office with their chickens in their hands as if they were holding trophies. When they passed the desk where the printed materials from the seminar were placed, they took a few pages to wrap the chickens. Before long, the pages were gone.

When the project leader told me that he had difficulties sending people on business trips, I didn't fully understand him, but now I could see why he was worried. The communist government had banned all religions in China and demanded absolute loyalty from the Chinese people. During the Cultural Revolution, many people had feverishly followed Mao's orders and participated in the violent purge. Only after Mao's death had they realized that the political movement had been a catastrophe and that they had wasted 10 years of their lives. Now the chickens in their hands meant more to them than national pride, communist ideology, or the project that was supposed to fill a void for the country.

Because the institute couldn't provide housing for the new employees, it only hired new graduates whose families lived in Beijing. All five new graduates in our group lived with our families in the city and commuted to work. Renting a place was unheard of at the time.

Every day, I left Mother's apartment at seven o'clock in the morning and took two buses to go to work. I didn't get home until seven o'clock in the evening. The long commute, along with the inability to go home during lunch break, was a disadvantage for new graduates. The institute promised us that new apartment buildings would soon be under construction and the housing shortage would be lessened.

When the new apartments were completed, however, they were assigned to male employees who had come to work before the Cultural Revolution. An official explained that the new graduates were not assigned apartments because "the older employees' apartments are too old and too small for their growing families and, therefore, they need the new apartments," and the reason that female employees didn't get new apartments was that "they can live in their husbands' apartments."

This decision caused discontent among females and the new graduates because part of the funding for the apartments' construction was deducted from everyone's income, not just that of the older males.

After lunch that day, the new graduates gathered in the office.

"In developed countries," a young man with broad shoulders said, "if a company provides housing to some employees, the other employees get monetary compensation." He sat on his desk and let his legs dangle.

"That sounds fair," I said, sitting by my desk across the room.

"It has been two years since we came to work here," the young man continued to rant, "but we have had no pay raise, no apartment, and no job title." He raised his voice, and his face turned red. We worked as engineers, but we couldn't call ourselves engineers without the institute giving us the title of engineer. So far, no one had received the title. Without it, our salary stayed low.

"Hopefully, we can all get an apartment one day, even the female employees," a woman with glasses said. She lived in her husband's apartment and commuted to work every day. "After all," she said, "the official promised us that more apartments would be built." She glanced in my direction, seeking support.

I nodded. I was in a steady relationship with a young man at the time; however, it didn't seem that we would have our own apartment anytime soon. The relationship would eventually fail, although the lack of our own place was not the only reason.

After other new graduates went to their desks to take a nap, I took out a physics book and started reading. I had applied to become a visiting researcher to work in America.

I'd heard of the program when an employee from the institute had gone to America as a visiting researcher not long before. In the program, qualified researchers, engineers, or college teachers could work in their fields in America or Canada for two years and then return to their work in China. To qualify, one had to work for two years after graduation from college and pass an English test as well as another test of his or her choice.

America was a country of mystery. We had grown up condemning her, yet we knew she was a place that attracted people from all over the world. In post–Cultural Revolution China, the government toned down its criticism of America. It was said that a top leader in post-Mao China had once admitted: "The countries that followed America have all become prosperous." In the 1980s, the educated people and college students looked to the West to find solutions to fix China's problems. Books on Western-style business management became popular. Names like Carnegie or Rockefeller were dropped during conversations among young people. Night after night, people in Beijing Concert Hall would not leave until John Phillip Sousa's "The Stars and Stripes Forever" was played.

I was disappointed by the situation at the institute. The unfair policy that denied female employees the right to an apartment was just one of many examples of the unreasonable treatment we had to endure. I told myself that there had to be other ways of doing things—more logical and reasonable ways. I wanted to see America for myself.

After I was accepted by the visiting researcher program, I, along with 30 other visiting researchers, was sent to a school in southern China to improve my English.

Enclosed by dark gray stone walls, the school sat on a wide street shaded by mature sycamores. A few two-story buildings overlooked an outdoor basketball court in the middle of the campus. My dorm room was on the second floor at the end of the building. It rained a few days after I arrived. The raindrops hit the window quietly. I sat on my bed and watched. Outside the window, a group of doves flew in a circle in the rain. I watched them for a long time and listened to the sound from the whistles fastened to their legs. I found the brave birds flying in the rain inspirational.

During the daytime, we had classes where we listened to English dialogs or a short story on tape and then took a test to see how much we understood. There was a cafeteria on campus where we had meals, but one of my classmates and I often left school to buy wonton soup in an elderly couple's tiny restaurant or have chicken noodle soup at a food stand on the street. On these "hunting trips," as we called them, we walked under the broad leaves of the sycamores with our enamel lunch boxes in hand. The metal spoons made a happy sound inside the boxes as we walked. I felt as if I were a college student again and my future was unknown but promising.

Our food-hunting trips stopped when my classmate was unexpectedly taken out of the visiting researcher program.

Unbeknownst to us, soon after our arrival in southern China to improve our English, someone back in Beijing had protested that co-workers, not just test results, should decide who could become a visiting researcher. We had no idea that while we were taking English classes in southern China, our qualifications as visiting researchers were being reevaluated back in Beijing. Our peers were asked to give their opinions of us. My classmate had been taken out of the program as a result.

"It was my project leader's idea to take me out of the program," my classmate said when we met again in Beijing later. By then, enough time had passed, and she sounded calm. I felt sorry for her. Some doves were not allowed to fly.

Although I stayed in the program, I was shaken by the event. It was disturbing that the authorities hadn't honored our agreement, but more shocking was the tactic of "behind-the-back evaluation," which had often been used during the Cultural Revolution as a means of "mass dictatorship." In the years immediately after the Cultural Revolution, a person's political standing, family background, and popularity were not nearly as important as his or her performance, and that was how I, along with many young people, had been able to go to college, get a good job, and be accepted into the visiting researcher program. I was afraid that the painfully familiar "supervision by the masses" was coming back. The Cultural Revolution had ended, but the mentality, the means, and the culture continued.

A few weeks later, I came back to Beijing and continued to work at the institute. At the same time, I sent out letters to universities in America, looking for a researcher position. Every day, I eagerly waited for responses.

One morning, when I walked into my office, I saw a note on my desk. It was from the department of education in the institute. It asked me to stop contacting foreign universities immediately. Puzzled, I went to the fourth floor, where the department of education was located.

Sitting behind her desk, a middle-aged woman with thin, straight hair informed me that the government's policy had changed. In a monotone voice, she told me that now a college graduate needed to work six years after school before she could leave China.

"The country has cultivated college graduates; in return, college graduates must make a contribution to the country." She sounded as if she were reading *People's Daily*.

"Is this just for visiting researchers?" I asked.

"No, the policy is for all college graduates unless you have relatives overseas—an uncle or an aunt."

"That means I have to wait another four years before I can leave," I said, feeling disappointed. *How can anyone plan her life under these ever-changing rules?* I thought to myself. I was resentful. A popular saying came to mind: "The Communist Party is like the sun: it brightens everywhere;

the party policy is like the moon: it changes every night."

"Not just wait, but work," she corrected me, patiently chewing a piece of candy. "You know that during the evaluation of your qualification as a visiting researcher, two of your colleagues from your group walked from the first floor to the seventh floor, telling everyone who would listen what a hardworking person you were, and that is why you were not taken out of the program. Don't change that," she warned.

"Oh, by the way," she continued, "you will not work overseas for two years anymore. You will work there for only one year. The country changed its policy on that, too."

I returned to my office and sat down at my desk, feeling drained, like a marathon runner about to finish the race only to find that the finish line has been moved farther away. The government changed its policy all the time, and people had to adapt. I was bitter.

Two female co-workers stood by a big table under a window, making a popular snack—tea egg. It was a lengthy, noisy process. First, they needed to make hard-boiled eggs in a pot on an electric plate. After that, they would tap the eggs with a spoon to crack the shell. They would then boil the eggs in salt and tea leaves until the eggs had brown, cracked patterns, giving them a desirable appearance. While waiting for the eggs to boil, the women chatted. They were discussing a female co-worker's basal body temperature.

"Her temperature should rise once a month, but it doesn't, and that's why she can't get pregnant," one woman said. She sounded concerned.

To control the population, not only did the government allow only one child per couple, but it also dictated when the baby could be born. Each year, only one of the employees in our department was allowed to get pregnant. Anyone who became pregnant without permission would be punished, although I didn't know the form of punishment because no one dared to get pregnant without permission. A woman in our group received approval to have a baby that year but had difficulty conceiving. Now she was receiving fertility treatments. If she couldn't become pregnant this year, she would use the only permission of the department for the next year. There were a couple of young married women in our department waiting for their turn to have a baby, and that was why the woman's basal temperature had become everyone's concern.

In the past, I hadn't participated in the activity of making tea eggs because I'd thought our office, which doubled as a lab, should be dedicated to the single purpose of our project, but now I felt differently. In a nation where a person couldn't decide when to leave the country and when to have a child, it seemed silly to worry about our ambitious project. I got up and joined the women. We chatted and laughed. The room was filled with the aroma of tea leaves, and the tapping of spoons meeting the eggshells sounded like a protest.

I worked another four years at the institute.

Many things happened in those years. After all the old graduates were assigned new apartments, more buildings were built, which gave the new graduates hope. However, again, the new apartments were assigned to the older male employees. This time, the new apartments were for their teenage children. The teenagers from two different families would share one apartment as their dorm rooms, which allowed more space in their parents' apartments.

Finally, I was allowed to leave China. On the last day at work, I sat down with the project leader at the same table where we'd sat on my first day at work six years earlier.

He wished me luck on my new adventure in America, and I thanked him for his support. I was sincere because he could have easily taken me out of the visiting researcher program for a good reason. At the time, we worked six days a week. In the past few weeks, when the Communist Party members in the institute had had meetings every Saturday afternoon, I would skip work and go home. I had grown frustrated by the communists' discriminative policies. The

Communist Party members had the advantage in every aspect of our lives: getting a promotion, a raise, or a ration coupon for a piece of furniture. If a non-party member committed a crime, he would be punished with prison time, while a party member would often be stripped of his party membership without serving time in jail for doing the same thing. I felt I didn't need to work if the party members didn't. Someone had warned me that the project leader was aware of my skipping work. I waited for him to talk to me and planned to use the opportunity to vent. Somehow the talk never happened, and the project leader didn't take me out of the visiting researcher program, either.

"You have worked very hard in the past six years," he told me as we said goodbye to each other.

I felt a tightness in my throat. I felt defeated. Four years earlier, when I'd entered the visiting researcher program, my primary goal had been to see America. Now, four years later, my leaving China felt like an escape. When the Cultural Revolution ended, I'd had hopes for China and myself. I'd done what I thought would lead to a happy life: going to college, working in the field I was trained for, and getting married. However, my effort hadn't led to happiness.

I had lost faith in post–Cultural Revolution China. I'd witnessed extreme corruption and injustice. Mao was dead, but the communists still ruled the nation. Abusing power was the norm. People without power were victimized by it, but as soon as they gained power, they abused it, too. It was a vicious cycle to which I couldn't see an end.

The project leader must have been disappointed, too.

The project was nowhere near completion, yet the research group was dissolving as a result of people leaving. Although the project leader banned anyone from leaving his team to pursue an advanced degree, among the five graduates who had joined the group the year I had, I was the last one to leave. The government, which had prohibited people from making money on their own for decades, now encouraged a portion of the population to "get rich first." As a result, people had more freedom to find jobs on their own or even have their own businesses.

At age 30, my future was foggy. I was about to spend a year in America, but I couldn't see what would happen after that.

CHAPTER FOURTEEN

1988 - 2001

In the early fall of 1988, I left China for America.

It was the first time I'd ever stepped on a plane. I followed a long line of passengers negotiating their way through the narrow aisle, trying to find their seats or an overhead compartment for their luggage. Some passengers were already seated. Most of them were Chinese. They sat quietly and almost solemnly, as if waiting for a big event to happen.

Flying was a big deal for Chinese people. We'd lived like trees under Mao. The government's household registration system had dictated that we live, work, and die in the same place where we were born. Traveling abroad had been almost impossible. Anyone who'd wanted to leave China had been considered a traitor. It was only after Mao was dead that getting a passport became possible, although it was very difficult.

I found my seat in the middle section of the plane and settled down. Through the small window, I could see the concrete pavement of the airport and workers loading luggage.

When the plane moved forward, my heart was pounding.

I had been preparing for this day for quite some time. Now that the moment was here, I felt mixed emotions of sadness, anxiety, and excitement. The day before, I had climbed the hills in the center of Beijing to say goodbye to my hometown. I'd wanted to see the golden tiles of the palaces in the Forbidden City glistening under the blue sky. However, the smog was so dense that I couldn't even see the ancient palaces across the street from me, and the blue sky that had often intoxicated me when I was a child was nowhere to be seen.

The plane shuddered and made loud noises as it accelerated. Eventually it lifted off the ground.

It was a 17-hour flight, and I didn't eat anything because I was too nervous. When a flight attendant asked me what she could offer me, I pointed at a bottle on her cart. I later learned the sweet water was called 7UP.

Like most Chinese, my understanding of America and its people was limited. I knew that America was a powerful country with advanced technology, but the Chinese government told us that capitalism had made the people greedy and cold to each other. At the visiting researcher orientation, someone had told us, "In America, if you are robbed, which could happen, don't shout 'Help,' because Americans don't care. You should scream 'Fire' instead. That's how you catch people's attention. Fire affects everyone."

The airplane cruised smoothly above the clouds, but I had a knot in my stomach. I worried about whether I could catch the connecting flight on time. I had no idea where I was staying my first night in America. I wasn't sure if American people would understand my English, because I had never spoken to a native English speaker before.

The following day, I got off the airplane at Los Angeles International Airport in the early afternoon. After going through customs, I rushed to find a transfer flight to Denver, Colorado.

The English broadcast through loudspeakers at the airport was much faster than the English I'd learned from the tapes or my teachers. Unlike in China, where everyone had black or gray hair, here, red, brown, or yellowish hair bobbed up and down in the hallway. Finding myself in a completely different environment, I felt like an intruder. *What am I doing here?* I asked myself, but I didn't have the time to dwell on the thought. I needed to catch the next flight if I was to arrive at my final destination of Fort Collins before dark. When I found the right gate in time and got on a plane that would take me to Denver, I breathed a sigh of relief.

It seemed that I was the only Chinese on this small airplane. Many passengers were young men wearing dark business suits. It was my first close-up observation of Americans. I noticed that they talked softly but laughed loudly.

At the Denver airport, I took a shuttle van to Fort Collins, a small town about 60 miles north. The driver of the white van stood by the door, greeting the passengers.

He must have been in his sixties, tall and with gray hair. His belly bulged under his crisp white uniform. He smiled and helped us with our luggage. As soon as I settled in the van, I noticed a small sign above the windshield. It read, "Tips are appreciated." A cardboard box was placed on the floor by the door. The sign and the box were evidence of capitalism, and I found them offensive.

Tips were not allowed in China. It was considered degrading to the receivers. When I was in China, store clerks were among the rudest people, and waiters in restaurants would sweep the floor when patrons were still eating. Still, we believed that in China, people were more equal than in the U.S. and that the working people, who were the masters of the nation, were more dignified than their counterparts in capitalist countries.

When the shuttle stopped at a small town, the driver got out of the vehicle, taking a small stepping stool with him. He bent over to place the stool on the ground in front of the door. A young woman got off the shuttle, stepped on the stool, and walked away in bouncy steps while the driver's gray hair fluttered in the wind.

We got back on the freeway, streaming along with other vehicles like fish in a river. Farther away, I saw only open land and big trees. There were no people. I felt homesick.

By the time I stepped off the van in front of a hotel in Fort Collins, the setting sun had painted the world golden, and the shadows of trees stretched across the lawn.

I made a phone call to the research lab where I was going to work and was told that someone would pick me up.

I stood on the steps of the hotel and waited.

Before long, a Chinese man in a dark gray button-down shirt appeared. He told me that he was a researcher at the lab. He didn't have a car, so we each carried one of my suitcases and walked for about 10 minutes to a big, old house covered with English ivy and chipped white paint.

We didn't enter the house by the front door; instead, we walked to the side. Four young Chinese men were sitting outside the window at a wooden table, chatting. They paused briefly when they saw us before continuing their animated discussion. I assumed they were graduate students who rented the house.

We walked through a side door into the house and stood in the middle of a kitchen. The floor was covered with blue and white tiles. A black wooden table stood in the middle, and a few mismatched chairs sat around it. On the left-hand side, under the window, was a sink. An electric rice cooker stood next to the sink on a tiled kitchen counter.

A young Chinese woman with glasses came out from another room and told me that they had just finished dinner but had some leftovers. She had me sit at the table. Only now did I realize that I hadn't eaten for more than 24 hours. The knot in my stomach had disappeared, and a feeling of hunger gripped me. The woman brought a bowl of white rice and a stir-fried vegetable dish and put them in front of me. I started eating right away. The woman went back to her room without saying anything. She must have been used to feeding newcomers because of the location of the house. Later, I couldn't remember much about the woman except her long ponytail and her slim shoulders when she turned around to scoop rice out of the rice cooker. I assumed she was a graduate student or the wife of one of the students I had seen outside the house.

While I was eating, the man who'd met me at the hotel made a few phone calls to see if any Chinese were looking for a roommate. Around nine o'clock that evening, a Chinese couple came in a small red car to pick me up. The man was a graduate student. He and his wife wanted to rent a room to me.

My new roommates were in their mid-twenties, thin, pale, and soft-spoken. The man wore glasses, and the woman had tied her straight hair into a short ponytail. They told me that their English names were Steven and Jenny.

"We are going west now," Steven said while looking ahead at the road. "I am driving slowly so that you know where we live."

"You don't need to remember all the street names," Jenny said, turning from the passenger seat to look at me. "Just remember the first letter of each street at the intersections. That way, you know how to get home: turn left at M and then turn right at L. That's how I found my way around when I first got here."

The car entered a quiet residential area where soft light beamed from the windows of rowhouses. Jenny said that the houses belonged to the university and were rented to graduate students for a reasonable rent. We parked the car in a parking lot and walked, passing four or five rows of houses before we came to the couple's unit.

Steven turned on a floor light with a yellow shade. The room was bare and somewhat dark. I attributed the darkness to two red brick walls. A small beige and brown plaid couch was placed against the wall facing the door, and a wooden coffee table sat in front of the couch. I didn't see any bed. Jenny said that this was a living room and that the bedrooms were separate. This was different from every home I had seen in Beijing. We had a housing shortage, and every room served as a bedroom, living room, studio, and sometimes dining room.

I didn't sleep well on my first night in America. I was jetlagged, and the moon was big and bright. The moonlight poured through the thin window curtain, washing the room white. Each time I fell asleep, a thought would jump into my head and wake me up: "I am in America now." It was an incredible feeling to sleep in a former enemy's land; it felt as if I had just landed on the moon.

The next day was a Saturday. In the morning, a few Chinese students and researchers crammed into three cars and headed for some garage sales. A few hours later, Jenny brought home a stack of white china, and I came back with a painting of flowers. I wanted to dress up the brick wall so that it wouldn't look so barren and rough.

That afternoon, I wrote a 10-page letter to Mother. I

described the flight, my new home, and my new roommates. I told her about my observations and thoughts since I'd left China. I spent four pages condemning what I'd seen on the shuttle van from Denver to Fort Collins: "How could they let a gray-haired man beg for tips? Where was the dignity? It hurt so much to see an elderly person bend down to place a stool on the ground for a woman young enough to be his granddaughter. This is what capitalism does to people; everything is about money." Although through Father's tragedy, I'd recognized the barbaric nature of the Communist Party, my value system had been established under communism, and I still believed that money was evil and the rich made the poor suffer.

Later in the afternoon, Steven and Jenny set up a dining table in the middle of the living room. They covered the table with a black and white checkerboard tablecloth and placed the white china on it. They told me that they had invited an American couple for dinner that night and wanted me to join them.

The guests were young and had a newborn baby. It was a quiet evening, and everyone talked softly. The baby fell asleep in the father's arms. When the mother took the baby from the father, he said to her, "Thank you." I have since forgotten the couple's names, and their faces have faded in my memory, but I could never forget the moment when I witnessed a husband thanking his wife. I wanted to know more about Americans.

After dinner, Jenny told me how to find local people who were willing to help foreign students and researchers in their new country. The next day, I went to an office at the university and left my contact information.

❧

A few days later, I was invited to a small birthday party for a young American man. Inside a house behind a white picket fence on a tree-lined street, I met four Americans: a woman in her thirties with big bright eyes and short blond hair; the woman's daughter, a five-year-old wearing a pink outfit; the birthday boy, who was in his twenties; and his friend, who had broad shoulders and a thick chest and was about the same age. The house was comfortably furnished. At the center of the living room was a coffee table with a glass top. Two big green couches were placed next to the coffee table, facing each other. At the end of the living room was a dining room, and beyond it was a kitchen.

At dinnertime, we sat around a square table in the dining room by the kitchen.

The woman, who was the hostess of the party, put a few small bottles of soft drinks in front of me. She pointed at each of them and told me the names of the drinks. She wanted me to try them all because I had just come from China and had never tasted most of them. Before we started to eat, we held hands and told the others the best thing that had happened during the day. The smiling faces and the friendly atmosphere relaxed me. The Americans were not as scary as they were portrayed to be by the Chinese media; on the contrary, they were what I'd hoped they would be— warm, friendly, and caring.

Just as I thought I had the Americans figured out, the young man with a thick chest said, "I made some money today that I don't have to pay taxes on." He looked around with a grin on his face, soliciting admiration. Everyone cheered.

I couldn't believe that the young man would reveal such a selfish, unpatriotic thought and that others would support him. I was used to confessing my selfish thoughts in criticism and self-criticism meetings in China, and I would hide the very bad ones.

After dinner, we sat at the dining table and chatted. The two young men didn't say much. They bit their fingernails and listened. Once in a while, the woman and her daughter ran their fingers across the top of the leftover birthday cake and then licked the icing off. I watched them with amazement. Americans didn't seem to have many rules. They were not guarded. They spoke at will, and they acted the way they, not the government or society, considered appropriate. They were free.

I didn't often see the American professor for whom I worked; instead, I worked with other Chinese researchers every day in the lab. They were in a similar situation as I was: researchers who would work in the lab for a year and go back to China afterward.

When I was alone in the lab, surrounded by electronic equipment that buzzed on the shelves by the walls, I felt a sense of coldness that no painting of flowers could fix. In China, I'd had similar feelings and had questioned my choice of profession from time to time. Now, being in a foreign country and an unfamiliar environment, the feeling was even more profound.

Colorado Springs is located 130 miles south of Fort Collins. I visited it when a church offered international students and researchers a free weekend trip. A bus took us from Fort Collins. About two and a half hours later, the bus slowed. An older gentleman, who was from the church that had organized the trip, stood up from his seat in the front of the bus. He told us that we were about to see a wonder called the Garden of the Gods. "It is magic," he said. "You will see some amazing rock formations with beautiful colors." His eyes twinkled with childlike excitement.

Our bus rolled off the main road and stopped in a parking lot. Outside the window, vertical red rocks dotted the landscape, majestic against the blue sky. Some passengers got off the bus. When it was half-empty, I looked around to find that none of the Chinese had left the bus.

"Isn't this a bit of an exaggeration? 'Garden of the Gods'?" a young man said, looking out the window.

"No comparison to our Yellow Mountain," another man agreed.

Someone recited a poem from the Ming dynasty: "It is not worth my while to look at another mountain after returning from Yellow Mountain."

While other people wandered around the rocks and stretched their cramped legs, we sat in the bus, immersing ourselves in a great sense of national pride enhanced by distance and homesickness.

The next stop was the Air Force Academy. We broke into a few smaller groups. Our group consisted of six Chinese. Our tour guide was a handsome young man in a pristine air force uniform. His black leather shoes were so shiny that they reflected Cadet Chapel like a mirror. After we passed the striking structure made of 17 spires, we came upon a flat field in front of some rowhouses and saw about a dozen men and women walking in a circle. I assumed they were doing marching practice, but I noticed these people were dragging their feet and hanging their heads. Other people in our group saw the strange scene, too.

"What are they doing?" someone asked the tour guide.

"They are being punished," the young man answered.

"Why?"

"Because they violated the rules."

"How is walking a punishment?" someone asked.

I had the same question. In China, a punishment involved

beating or doing hard labor. We marched in elementary school often; it was never a punishment. We were told that marching was a good thing. Hardship built character.

"Today is Saturday," the tour guide said, smiling and showing his white teeth. "These people could have been going to the movies or seeing their girlfriends. Instead, they are here because they broke the rules. They lost their freedom, and that's the punishment."

Losing freedom was a punishment; that was a new concept. In China, we were told that our lives belonged to the country. In the giant machine of our great socialist motherland, we were supposed to be a tiny bolt willing to shine wherever the government needed us. We never had freedom and never dared to ask for it. Wanting personal freedom meant rejecting the Communist Party's leadership, which was dangerous.

❧

During the first few months in America, the feeling of loneliness never left me. At night, I dreamed about every person that I had known—my family members, my friends, even the people I'd known in kindergarten but had lost contact with over the years. I enjoyed chatting and laughing with Steven and Jenny. However, as soon as they walked out the door, the apartment would become quiet, and a sense of emptiness would engulf me. Before long, I moved out and rented a semi-basement apartment from an elderly American couple. I'd rather be alone all the time to avoid the emotional roller coaster.

My new landlords lived in a two-story, colonial-style house with white siding and a gray gabled roof. The wide front door had elegant stained-glass sidelights on each side. Inside the door was a big living room with a shiny hardwood floor and a few area rugs. A few pots of tall green houseplants enlivened the space. I lived downstairs in the semi-basement. I had my own bathroom, kitchen, bedroom, and a small window situated up high on the living room wall. From the window, I couldn't see the sky, but I could see the ground, a road, people's feet, and dogs' legs.

I called the landlady Erka until I realized her name was Erica. She was a petite lady, just over five feet tall. Her hair was dark, with a slight natural wave, just long enough to cover her ears. She talked and walked fast. She told me that she belonged to a senior swimming club.

Behind the house and surrounded by a wooded area was a big lawn. Erica's husband, a retired lawyer for a bank, cut the grass with a riding lawnmower, making the green lawn as smooth as a carpet. Once in a while, a gray rabbit would leap out from the woods and hop about on the grass.

One afternoon, I came home from the lab and saw Erica kneeling on the lawn. Her purple shirt caught my eye. I thought she had fallen and couldn't get up. I ran over to her.

"Erka, Erka," I called out.

"What is it?" She looked up from underneath her straw hat. She seemed to be fine.

"What are you doing?" I asked.

"Pulling weeds." She pointed at a red plastic bucket next to her. It had weeds in it.

"You can join me if you'd like," she said, standing up. "You can do yard work anytime you want. You should keep a log for yourself and deduct four dollars and 25 cents for each hour you've worked when it is time to pay your rent."

I looked at her, wondering if I should feel offended. I was an educated researcher, and now she wanted me to work as a laborer for my rent?

On the campus in Beijing, the milkwoman would clank her gong on Sundays, urging the residents to come out and pull weeds or sweep the roads. During the Cultural Revolution, however, these activities had been done by the class enemies. While pulling weeds, they would face a wall or away from the roads. They were ashamed. Physical labor was a punishment.

I changed into a pair of dark pants and joined the landlady. We were on our hands and knees, crawling all over and pulling weeds. We also worked at a planter in front of the house next to the street. When some neighbors walked by, Erica chatted with them. She didn't seem to be embarrassed that her neighbors saw her digging in the dirt.

I did more yard work, sometimes alone and sometimes with Erica. It helped me pay rent. The minimum wage was $4.25 an hour at the time. I didn't negotiate with Erica. As a matter of fact, I appreciated her setting the rate; I'd have been embarrassed if I'd had to talk about money. In China, the subject of money was taboo. Money was a symbol of capitalism. We didn't want to talk about it because it made us look greedy, yet we couldn't live without it.

It seemed that things were much simpler for the Americans; money didn't have to be dirty, and doing physical labor didn't have to be a sign of a failed life.

It didn't take me long to realize that I wanted to stay in America as long as possible. I liked the nation that I'd started to know. The American people and their logical way of thinking and common sense intrigued me. Their freedom to express themselves was what I yearned for. In America, desiring and pursuing personal happiness was one's right. Here, human nature was acknowledged, accepted, and respected instead of being suppressed. More importantly, the situation in China was worrisome. In 1966, Mao wrote to his wife about the Cultural Revolution that he had just launched two months before: "Reach great order through great chaos; repeat it in another seven or eight years." Mao was now dead, but China was not out of his shadow. The communists still ruled the nation and praised Mao as their great leader. I was afraid that another Cultural Revolution was around the corner.

Becoming a graduate student seemed to be the most logical way to stay in America legally. I took some required exams and sent out application forms to a few universities. I chose physics as my major because I needed a tuition scholarship. Only physics, math, and chemistry departments would hire foreign students as teaching assistants and grant them a tuition scholarship.

When I expressed my desire to extend my stay in America, I received an application form from the institute in Beijing. I was to fill it out and return it to get permission to stay in America beyond one year.

A few months after I had arrived in America, in April 1989, the Tiananmen Square student protests broke out. The Chinese people had been angry at the government for a long time. The recent death of a purged communist official, whom the people viewed as a reformer and a potential Chinese Mikhail Gorbachev, triggered the protests. The square was covered from end to end with people, flags, and banners. The students wanted freedom of the press and an end to government corruption. I watched the protests on TV every day with great interest because I understood the students' anger and was sympathetic toward them.

By mid-May, some students in the square began a hunger strike, and the crowd continued to grow. On May 20, the government declared martial law.

On June 4, I woke up and turned on the TV. The government had cracked down on the protesters with the military. I was stunned to see the images of the wounded men being placed on stretchers or flatbed tricycles and rushed off by others. One wounded young man wasn't on a stretcher or a tricycle. Instead, a few young men carried him by his arms and legs. He was rushed away from danger with his face up and his back only a few inches above the ground. He seemed to be unconscious. Fire painted the sky red, and people were running in every direction. I saw mangled bicycles with human bodies piled on them. I saw military men with rifles and helmets. They roared like animals as they charged forward. I couldn't understand what they were shouting. It was almost as if they were speaking a foreign language. I then saw the tanks.

I couldn't believe my eyes. The Chinese government was using tanks on the unarmed students. I wasn't surprised that the Chinese government would kill its own people. By now I had already figured out that Father's death had not been caused by Lin Biao alone. Instead, the Chinese communist government was responsible. Still, sending tanks to the square to crack down on a peaceful protest in front of the whole world was beyond my imagination.

Then I saw astonishing footage of a slim young man in a white shirt and dark pants standing in front of a long row of tanks on Tiananmen Square, trying to stop it from rolling forward. It was the day after the overnight crackdown. The square was free of protesters. I guessed that the young man was a Beijing resident. From time to time, he waved the jacket in his hand at the tanks. I couldn't see his face, but from his body language, I could sense his anger and profound sadness, and I felt the same way. I clenched my fists and cried out, "Get out of my city."

The peaceful student demonstration was crushed by the ruthless government and its military.

Somehow I still held on to a slim hope that Deng Xiaoping, the highest leader of the Chinese Communist Party at the time, was ignorant of the violence against the students due to his old age and that once he found out about the massacre, he would right the wrong. I soon found out how naïve I was. Not long after the Tiananmen Square massacre, Deng rewarded the military personnel who had been a part of the crackdown by taking photos with them. The event was televised. Deng was alert and jubilant, applauding and waving to the "heroes."

The tanks had broken the concrete pavement in Tiananmen Square and destroyed any hope that I had left for the communists.

When the graduate school at Marquette University in Wisconsin offered me a scholarship to study physics, I accepted it without hesitation.

After I purchased a Greyhound bus ticket to Wisconsin, I phoned the physics department at Marquette. A professor answered the call and handed the phone to a female Chinese graduate student who happened to be in the building. "Don't worry," she said in a sweet voice. "Call me from the Greyhound bus station when you get here. I will pick you up." She gave me her phone number. I told her the date and time that I would be there, along with my phone number. "I can find a place for you to stay until you find your own apartment," she added.

I arrived in Milwaukee, Wisconsin, on a cloudy day and called the Chinese girl from the bus station. However, the phone line was disconnected. I looked at the two suitcases standing on each side of me and decided to call the physics department. A woman answered. She introduced herself as the secretary of the department. She told me that the Chinese girl whom I had spoken with had left for another city. I glanced out the bus station window at the sky, which was as gray as a block of lead, and sighed. The secretary said she would find someone to pick me up. "It is summer break; not many people are here in the building," she said, "but I will see if I can find someone."

The secretary sent a middle-aged man with square shoulders and dark hair. After he shook my hand and put my luggage in the trunk of his car, we were on our way to the campus. He was not talkative, and I had a lot on my mind. The man stopped the car in front of the physics department building and helped me take the luggage into an office on the second floor. He then took off.

The secretary, an older woman with straight hair, stood behind a chest-high counter. From behind her glasses, her wide-eyed gaze revealed a youthful curiosity.

"You are not going to chew gum when you teach, are you?" she asked me. I had been hired by the physics department as a teaching assistant.

"Oh, no, of course not," I said. I chewed gum to cover up my nervousness.

"I couldn't find anyone here to get you except for the dean of the department," she said.

"Here." The woman pointed at an address on a piece of paper to get my attention while I was still trying to comprehend the fact that she had sent the dean of the department to pick me up at the bus station.

"Go take an English exam at this address," the woman said.

"Now?"

"Yes, now."

I looked at my luggage. I didn't know where I was staying that night.

"You can leave your luggage here," she said.

I moved the two suitcases to the corner of the room and left.

I rented an apartment on the second floor of a hundred-year-old red brick building. I liked it from the first time I stepped inside. The small room had white walls and light-colored carpet. The window was open, and a white curtain billowed in the wind, free like a bird.

Just as I was getting ready for my new life as a graduate student, I was told by the international student office at the university that my current non-student visa didn't allow me to work for the physics department and that I needed to obtain a student visa. Being unable to work for the physics department meant I would lose the tuition scholarship from the graduate school, which was offered only to people who would work for the departments. Without money for tuition and fees, I couldn't register as a student, which meant that I couldn't obtain a student visa while my current visa was expiring.

At about the same time, I received the form that I had filled out and sent to the institute in Beijing. On the returned form, someone had written a line in rushed handwriting: "The country has a longstanding rule that a visiting researcher is not allowed to become a graduate student."

What longstanding rule? I thought. I knew that the institute had allowed a visiting researcher to stay in America to pursue an advanced degree.

And who wrote this? I looked at the form and couldn't tell who had written the line or which department they worked in because there was no signature or name.

In China, the words "country" and "government" were interchangeable. No one took personal responsibility, and everyone, including the government, hid behind "the country." Everything was done for "the country" and by "the country," including the soldiers who'd shot at the students in Tiananmen Square and the ones who had killed Father. That was one of many reasons I wanted to stay in America. I tossed the form in the drawer.

Unwilling to return to China, where the government had just killed students in Tiananmen Square, I decided to fight for a chance to get into school. I talked to the administration office at the graduate school, the physics department, and the international student office. Nothing worked, and in the meantime, school registration had begun in a big white tent set up between two buildings.

On the last day of registration, a young professor from the physics department took me to see people he thought might help me. It was hot, and we walked on campus from building to building and visited office after office. He was tall and walked with big strides in front of me. Sweat dampened the back of his white shirt. By afternoon, it was clear that I was not going to be enrolled as a student.

"Why don't you talk to the dean?" he asked.

"I did." I thought he meant the dean of the department.

"No, I mean the dean of the graduate school."

"Really? Can I do that?"

If someone had given me this suggestion in China, I would have laughed at him, but this was America, where the school campus had no walls and the head of the department gave a ride to a student from a bus station. I decided to take the professor's advice, although I worried that time was running out.

The head of the graduate school saw me in his office immediately. He sat behind his desk, facing the door. He was in his late forties or early fifties and wore glasses. When I walked in, he stood up from his seat and shook my hand. From the big window behind him, I could see students were rushing to the tent where registration was to close in a few hours.

The man listened to my plea and read the papers I'd brought with me: transcripts from the university I'd attended in Beijing, an acceptance letter from Marquette, as well as a letter from the graduate school offering me a full-tuition scholarship.

"I just came back from Beijing and visited the university you attended. It is an excellent school," he said, looking up from the paper. "I am honored that you have chosen us."

He picked up a pen and wrote a few words on one of the documents in front of him.

"We will honor the scholarship that we offered you. Now, go get registered." He stood up, handed me the documents, and shook my hand.

I ran out the door, weeping.

Life as a foreign student was filled with hope, excitement, and, at times, awkwardness.

In class, I sat in the front row so that I could hear every word. I took notes in Chinese because I couldn't write fast enough in English. During the break, when other students walked by me on their way out of the classroom, they discovered my notes and stood around my desk, looking at my notebook as if they were studying unearthed artifacts. "Are you sure we attended the same class?" one teased me. I read English slowly. Before I finished reading one-third of a textbook, it was already time to take the final exam. Luckily, there was a lot of math involved in the exams, and math is a universal language.

After I received a student visa, I started to work for the department 20 hours a week. My duties included giving lectures to show the students how to solve physics problems, monitoring students' physics experiments, taking attendance for the professors, and so on.

⁓

As I was settling into my busy routine, China was not always in my thoughts. However, in the back of my mind, questions remained: why did the Cultural Revolution have to happen, and why did people have to die? As a human, I couldn't understand Mao's mindset.

One day, I was doing homework in a library on campus. My favorite place was on the third floor, where religion and political science books were kept. It was the least crowded floor.

When I took a break from physics, I walked between the bookshelves, picked up a book, and opened it. It was about

Mao and the Chinese people, "Mao's ants," as the author called us. The book relayed information from some Russian historians who said that Mao was not afraid of a nuclear war and believed that his country could survive one even if it lost 300 million people. The book revealed an incident in 1958 when Mao had proposed to the Soviets a plan to defeat the Americans: in a war, the Chinese forces would retreat to the central provinces, drawing American forces after them. At that point, "the Soviets would attack the Americans with everything you've got," Mao had said. He'd proposed a nuclear war on Chinese soil to kill Americans. He was willing to sacrifice Chinese people's lives so that he could become the leader of the post-war "unified world."

A light bulb went on in my head. The 10 minutes of reading had answered a decade-long question. The tens of millions of deaths under Mao were not "mistakes," as the government explained. They were intentional. The devil treated human beings as his leverage. We were nothing but Mao's pawns. We had no faces, no feelings, no families, and no dreams. Our only value was to support his regime and die for his ego.

I couldn't remember the title of the book, or maybe I didn't even look at it, but later I would read Mao's heartless proposal in the *New York Times* as well as in the Soviets' former foreign minister Andrei Gromyko's memoir, *Memories.*

The most efficient form of brainwashing is omitting facts. Mao's unthinkable plan had been exposed in front of the whole world, but it was not available to the Chinese. If I hadn't left China, I wouldn't have read about it, and I would have still been struggling to make sense of why a leader of a nation would make his people miserable.

෴

I was observing and learning both inside and outside of school, and I made adjustments. I stopped telling my students to "shut up" to get their attention at the beginning of a class. I also found out that I was not supposed to toss the plastic tray in the trashcan after I finished a meal at a fast-food restaurant as I had when I'd first come to America. As prosperous as America was, the plastic tray was not disposable, and the restaurant could use it for other patrons. As time went by, I became more comfortable and confident in this new country.

෴

A year had passed since I'd entered graduate school; now it was time to choose an academic advisor to guide me through my scientific research to receive a master's degree. I asked Prof. Kouris, who was the longest-serving faculty member in the department and had more than a hundred articles published in scientific journals, along with inventions and patents. In his early seventies, Prof. Kouris reminded me of a pre–Cultural Revolution Chinese educational film, in which a good-natured man with thinning white hair and a white mustache answered children's questions about science and nature. Children called the man Grandpa Knowledge. Grandpa Knowledge was later condemned as a representative of bourgeois academic authority during the Cultural Revolution, and the movie was banned.

Before we decided on the direction of my research, Prof. Kouris asked me to work with him in the lab to familiarize myself with the equipment and surroundings. When I watched him preparing samples for the experiment that he was doing for the chemistry department, I thought he'd ignored an important factor, but I didn't say anything.

At the end of the day, he was not pleased with the results of the experiment. "This can't be right," he said, lighting a cigarette.

That night, I thought about what had happened in the lab during the day and was certain that the professor had made an error in preparing the samples. It was not a big mistake; he'd simply forgotten something.

I was in a dilemma. I didn't want to point out the error because I didn't want to offend him. Pointing out a teacher's mistakes was to be avoided in China, and it was something that I had never done or witnessed because embarrassing a superior could have very bad consequences in a culture where saving face was everything. In China, a teacher was an authority figure whom one shouldn't challenge. Of course, during the Cultural Revolution, things were different.

During that period, saving face wasn't important; staying alive was. I hoped that the following day, Prof. Kouris would realize his error. If he didn't, I would find a chance to mention it casually in the subtlest way.

The next day in the late afternoon, after a day of teaching, my advisor came to the lab. The phone rang. It was the chemistry department asking about the results of the experiment. "I don't have them just yet," Prof. Kouris said and hung up the phone. He puffed a cigarette and frowned. I could tell he was agitated.

"Go home," he said to me. "There is no reason to stay here."

We walked out of the lab and down the hallway, which was getting dark. I stayed half a step behind him because I believed that was what a respectful student should do. Before we walked out of the building and went our separate ways, I gathered the courage to tell him that we hadn't considered the individual unit weight of the materials when preparing the samples. I didn't know how he would respond. It was a small error, but the smaller the error, the bigger the embarrassment to some people.

The professor stopped and slowly turned around to face me.

His eyebrows lifted, and his eyes brightened. He was smiling.

"You've made me happy," he said.

That Saturday, he took me to a Greek restaurant to have dinner with his family. I met Mrs. Kouris for the first time and fell in love with dolmades, a Greek dish made with grape leaves stuffed with a delicious mix of herbs and rice.

My experiment was going smoothly, and the professor was pleased. He believed I could start writing my thesis soon. "You will graduate on time," he said.

When the weather was calm, we would walk to a nearby restaurant to have lunch. We walked through campus, between the red brick buildings and among the young students. Strolling side by side, we enjoyed the sun, the breeze, and the sights and sounds. On those days, I often thought about Mother. She was an academic advisor to a graduate student in her university. I hoped Mother and her student got along as well as Prof. Kouris and I did.

Under my advisor's guidance, I finished my research and wrote a thesis.

The morning of my thesis defense, I came to the professor's office and sat in a chair across the desk from him. It was a glorious day; the sun shone through the window, landing on his white hair and brightening his face. "You should be proud of yourself," he said.

I graduated in the fall of 1992 and tried to find a job. The U.S. government now allowed the Chinese people who had come to America before or shortly after the 1989 Tiananmen Square massacre to work in the country so that we didn't have to go back to China to face possible persecution.

Eventually the U.S. government would grant us green cards.

The nation was, however, in a recession. Jobs in physics were difficult to find. To support myself, I worked as a shipping clerk, a technician, and eventually in the computer field. To save money, I rented a room in a house and shared a kitchen with my landlords. Although I faced difficulties, I hoped for a better future, and I enjoyed freedoms that I'd never had in China. I got my driver's license and drove around in an old Buick with a crushed front grille and a missing headlight. The car didn't want to start on cold mornings and would stall when I waited at red traffic lights, but once she started, she charged forward so fast that she left all other cars in the dust. I often had my window down and let my hair dance in the wind.

The following year, in a little corner store called The Bakery, I met my future husband. On our first date, we had lunch at an Italian restaurant. Bill was late, but I forgave him as soon as I spotted the bouquet of flowers in his hands. Tall, slim, and wearing glasses, he sported a light blue button-down shirt and a pair of black jeans. He brought with him a book, *Art and Physics*. Over spaghetti and meatballs, we talked and talked. He had trusting eyes and a soothing voice. I found the American man before me not only attractive but also intelligent.

The next day we went to the beach. Sitting on the sand side by side, we watched white waves tirelessly rushing to the shore and pelicans silently gliding under the blue sky.

I felt relaxed. It had been five years since I came to America. I had received my degree, moved to California, found a job, and settled down. During the process, I'd transformed from someone who was overwhelmed when facing choices into a confident person who was not afraid to make my own decisions. Life was good, and I wanted someone to share it with.

Two years later, on a beautiful summer morning, we had our wedding in a park overlooking the Pacific Ocean. It was still early, and the park was quiet. Under a palm tree, a string quartet in black tuxedos tested their instruments as our friends and Bill's family gradually showed up. When the music rose, I stepped down a path lined by palm trees and covered with green grass. Wearing a white wedding gown and holding a bouquet of roses, I walked toward Bill, who stood next to the minister, waiting for me. Our friends were smiling, and onlookers were watching.

I walked alone.

Bill, looking handsome in his tuxedo, left the minister behind and walked toward me. When we met, he turned and offered his left arm. Together, we walked toward the minister. After we exchanged the marriage vows and wedding rings, the minister announced that we were husband and wife.

It was a perfect wedding, except that my family was absent. I hadn't invited them.

Three years earlier, immediately after I moved to California, Mother had visited me. I rented her a quiet room on the first floor in the house where I lived. Outside the floor-to-ceiling window of Mother's room was a beautiful rose garden. There, she saw hummingbirds for the first time. We went to the movies, stores, and the beach. I took her to

Disneyland and SeaWorld.

Six months later, Mother went back to China. I saw her off at the airport. I watched as she hesitantly navigated through the unfamiliar territory of an international airport. When her petite figure disappeared into the crowd, I felt more than sadness; I was angry.

After Mother had arrived from Beijing, she told me that because she'd come to see me, she had lost her position as a professor at two universities and had been forced into retirement by the government. The year was 1993, and a passport was a tool for the government to control people. Mother was told that she had to resign from all her jobs to receive the passport. "It is government policy," an official told her. The government's reasoning was that since Mother had an opportunity to stay in the U.S., she should make her positions available for someone else. So, to see me, Mother had to give up what she loved: teaching. I felt guilty and didn't want my family to make more sacrifices just to attend my wedding.

∾

The morning of September 11, 2001, was eerily quiet. I was stepping out of our house to pick up the newspaper when my neighbor walked over and asked, "Did you see it on TV?" I shook my head.

"Did you notice there are no planes in the sky?" he asked.

"You're right," I said, looking up. "What happened?"

"Turn on the TV, and you'll see," he said, walking away.

I turned on the TV and couldn't believe my eyes: dark smoke was pouring out from two tall buildings. A few terrorists had hijacked two airplanes and flown them into the buildings of the World Trade Center in New York, killing almost 3,000 people.

The hatred-infused people had done the unthinkable to the American people.

I felt anger and pain.

The means the terrorists had used to kill innocent people were shocking, but equally shocking was the reaction of many Chinese people. Shortly after the attack, I read that upon hearing of the incident, some Chinese college students poured into the streets of Beijing to celebrate. Some Chinese people even cheered and applauded in an airport in the U.S. while watching the Twin Towers collapsing on TV. They were more excited than they'd been at winning the 2008 Olympic bid.

I was deeply disappointed. From the student protest for democracy in Tiananmen Square to the student celebration of a terrorist attack, only 12 years had passed. China's economic achievement had validated the tyrannical regime. The decades-long "patriotism education" by the Chinese government had created an environment where a big portion of the population saw foreigners as threats and enemies, especially Westerners and the Japanese.

The year before the September 11 attack, I had become an American citizen. I accepted American values and appreciated American culture; however, even after I became an American citizen, I still aligned myself with the Chinese people culturally and emotionally because I had grown up in China and I thought I understood my people. The joyous response to the September 11 terrorist attack from some Chinese people changed that. Now I saw a gap between my view and that of many Chinese people.

This eye-opening event made me realize that people from the same ethnic background don't always think or act alike. Birthplace doesn't decide who we are. A true individual answers to his or her own conscience and follows his or her own judgment. This realization allowed me to finally think freely.

CHAPTER FIFTEEN

2010

Twenty-two years had passed since I'd come to America, and China had become a distant memory.

When I'd left China, I hadn't brought one photo with me. The past was too painful to revisit. For decades, to go on with my life, I'd tried not to think about Father and his tragedy, but I knew at the most tender corner of my emotions lived the memory of Father and the pain caused by his death. In my happiest moments, I could hear the sadness in my laughter, and when I listened to music, tears often rolled down my face without reason.

In late summer, when I was on the way to Beijing to visit Mother as I had in the past, I had no idea that the carefully covered wound in my heart would be ripped open when my sister-in-law handed me the copy of the magazine pages that revealed the details of Father's death. Looking at her tearful eyes, I didn't have the courage to read the article. I put it in my suitcase and hid it in the closet of my hotel room.

After I returned to America, I put the copy of the article inside the book *China Builds the Bomb*. In the book, Father was listed as one of the key scientists of the Chinese nuclear weapons program. Mother had asked me to buy a copy for her when the book came out. By the time I was ready to send it to her, she did not want it anymore. Father's death had tormented her as much as it did me. After Father's death, she had been furious with Mao and the government, but in the past few years, she had changed. Not wanting the internal turmoil to destroy her life to the very last minute, she was trying to put out the flame of anger inside her. She didn't want the book to bring back painful memories.

A month passed, and I still hadn't read the article. I didn't want to derail my peaceful life, and I didn't know if I was strong enough to face the cruel facts.

It was Thanksgiving. At a small holiday gathering at a friend's house, I struck up a conversation with Don.

This American man in his mid-forties, tanned and in a light-colored, button-down shirt, leaned against the kitchen counter behind him with a glass of wine in his hand. A rectangular pendant light hung low above the granite island counter between us. Don spoke fluent Mandarin Chinese and had a master's degree in Chinese history. The topic of our conversation was China. When talking about the disastrous political movements by Mao, Don said, "Mao's intention was good."

"His intention was never good," I said without hesitation. "Mao did it for his own ego and power and was never for the people."

Don took his elbow off the kitchen counter and stood up straight.

"What you said is true," he said.

I was surprised that he retracted so quickly. It seemed he'd known all along that Mao had been a dictator who'd had no regard for his fellow human beings, but he hadn't wanted to offend me because I was Chinese.

"The 'intention theory' was a good one," I said, softening the tone of my voice. I was a little embarrassed by my strong reaction to his comment.

"It wasn't my invention; you should know," he said, smiling and looking down at his wine glass.

Of course, I knew. Claiming that its leader had good intentions was the communist government's way of legitimizing its control over the Chinese people. Some Chinese repeated the government's lie when they felt their collective pride was under attack.

On this joyous night, friends chatted and laughed. Outside the windows, the Pacific Ocean shimmered under the moon, and Catalina Island looked soft and elusive in the distance.

"You know," Don said, swirling the wine in his hand,

"Westerners use a double standard when it comes to the millions of people who died under Mao. Because the victims of Mao were Chinese, Westerners don't pay as much attention to what happened in China as, say, in Europe during World War II."

"One reason Mao is not recognized as a Stalin-like monster by the people in the world is that most Chinese people don't speak up about his crimes," I said.

"You're right," Don said. "Like the saying goes: 'Nothing has really happened until it has been recorded.' No matter how horrific the situation was, if not enough people talk about it, to outsiders, it didn't happen."

I didn't know what to say. It occurred to me that I was one of the Chinese people who'd witnessed the crimes but didn't speak up.

When I'd first left China, I'd naïvely thought that everyone in the world knew about the Cultural Revolution. How could they not? So many people had suffered and died. However, a few times when I'd talked about life in China, my American friends would ask, "Why didn't we know this before?" I'd even read some glowing reports by some American reporters visiting China in the early '70s, when the Chinese people had still been miserable during the Cultural Revolution. Due to a lack of information, the world didn't know the scale of the crimes committed by the communists, which had allowed the romantic fantasy of the illusionary classless, stateless world hypothesized by Karl Marx to continue to brew in some minds.

The next day, I took out the pages that my sister-in-law

had given to me in the hotel room in Beijing and sat down at a desk by the window in our living room. I decided to read the article. No matter how cruel the truth was, if Father had gone through it, as a daughter, I needed to know about it.

But I hesitated. My sister-in-law's tears in the hotel room had forewarned me about what I was about to read. Many people had died a horrendous death during the Cultural Revolution. A well-known case was a woman who had been imprisoned and tortured for having an anti-Cultural Revolution view. Before she'd been killed by the Chinese government, her throat had been slashed to prevent her from speaking. I read about a story where a kidney had been taken from a live political prisoner without anesthesia in 1970 before her execution. Was I going to read something that gruesome? Would I be able to handle it?

I put the pages down on the desk and looked out the window.

A giant bird of paradise plant stood proudly in the bright sun. Underneath the shade of the lush, leafy plant lay a little yellow feral cat that we had befriended. She was sleeping and didn't seem to have a worry in the world. For a moment, I wished I were that carefree cat. But sometimes we are forced to face difficult situations and make a decision that we'd rather not. Through the process, we fulfill our obligations, grow up, and mature.

I walked to the kitchen where my husband was preparing lunch. I wanted to talk to him and hear him tell me that I would be OK. I needed his support and encouragement. Facing the window, Bill didn't see me. I walked over and stood by him. We were so close; I could feel the warmth from his body. I looked at him but didn't say anything. No words were necessary.

I walked back to the living room, sat down by the window, and picked up the pages. *I will be OK,* I said to myself. Yes, it would be painful to read the article, and yes, I would be devastated. But I knew that I would be fine in the end, because the man who was making sandwiches in the kitchen would catch me when I fell and put the pieces back together when my heart was broken.

I took a deep breath and unfolded the pages.

It was an interview with a former party head of the Chinese Qinghai-based Nuclear Weapons Research and Design Academy in the Chinese nuclear weapons program. It was on the fourth page where I found the paragraph about Father:

> *Also tortured and killed during the Cultural Revolution by the rebels was our country's renowned explosives expert Qian Jin. After his death, on the surface, there were no obvious injuries, but an autopsy revealed that his organs had become bloody lumps. The evil rebels used a big iron rod, pressing his body like they were rolling out dough until he was crushed to death.*[1]

---

[1] Translated by Ying Qian

Like many people who spoke up about the crimes during the Cultural Revolution, Li Yingjie blamed the rebels. If he had pointed out that the criminals were military men, the article wouldn't have been published.

What I read shook me to the core. It took me a few times to read through the short paragraph in the article because my eyes kept glancing over the words. I was afraid that if I looked at them too long, what I read would become real.

I was shaking. What evil. What hatred. What cowards! To inflict maximum pain and, at the same time, leave the least amount of visible evidence, the Chinese military had chosen the most barbaric and personal way to kill my father, the gentlest and kindest man I have ever known.

I thought I was prepared before I read the article, but I wasn't. I cried, but there were no tears. The pain was so intense that it burned me inside. I couldn't breathe.

Decades before, on one rainy night, my neighbor Grandma Gao had told me a Chinese legend:

> *In ancient times, an emperor ordered the best blacksmith of the country to make a giant bronze bell for him. After three months, the bell was finished and presented to the emperor, who was delighted. However, at the first strike, the bell cracked. When melting bronze during the manufacturing of the bell, the blacksmith had not been able to raise the temperature high enough. The emperor was enraged, and the blacksmith was beheaded. A*

second blacksmith was brought in to make the bell. The bell cracked, and the blacksmith was beheaded. A third blacksmith was brought in, and then a fourth.

The emperor sent out officials to find blacksmiths from all over the country to make the bell for him. One of the blacksmiths was from deep in the mountains. When the family heard that the blacksmith had been asked to work for the emperor, they were worried. "To be in the emperor's company is tantamount to living with a tiger" is an ancient Chinese proverb. But the blacksmith had no choice. Resisting the emperor's order would be punishable by death.

The blacksmith followed the officials to the capital. With him was his daughter in her red outfit and red shoes. The blacksmith worked hard on the bell, but he couldn't get the temperature high enough. The deadline was approaching, and the blacksmith would be killed if he could not make the bell in time. Beside the giant furnace where the bronze was being heated, the officials and the executioners waited. The metal in the furnace was so hot it became liquid. The blacksmith knew the temperature was still not high enough to make a good bell. Sweat dripped down from his face, and his hands were shaking. His helpers worked frantically. The temperature didn't go up anymore. The blacksmith and his helpers lost hope and bowed their heads. At this moment, the daughter of the blacksmith walked toward the furnace. Calmly, she cut off her long black hair and tossed it in the furnace. A light smoke rose. Before anyone realized what was happening, the daughter jumped into the furnace, and a white cloud went up. The blacksmith rushed over, but he could only grab her red shoe. The temperature of the bronze increased. The bell was made, and the blacksmith's life was saved.

"The bell has been hanging in the bell tower in Beijing ever since," Grandma Gao said. "On stormy nights, the sound of the bell is especially sad. Mothers in Beijing tell their children, 'Listen, the bell lady is looking for her lost red shoe.'"

I didn't like the story and had tried to forget it, and for many years, I had. But now, after reading about Father's death, the story came to my mind. Given the opportunity, I would have done anything to spare Father from the pain he'd suffered and save his life, but I couldn't. I was not as lucky as the daughter of the blacksmith. I hadn't been there for him when he'd needed me. Father had died alone in the cold and barren plateau, surrounded by animals in human clothing. No matter what I did now, it would not bring him back.

But I can lend him a voice, I thought. Father cannot

talk anymore, but I can. I didn't and couldn't stop any crimes during the Cultural Revolution, but I can at least document them.

For years, I had avoided talking about Father because I didn't want to peel away the protective layers that covered the deep wound in my heart. For years, I had avoided thinking about the Cultural Revolution, the witch hunt that had taken away many lives and destroyed many families, because I wanted to have a normal life.

I felt ashamed. America had become a great country because its people took a stance when it mattered. Anyone who survives crimes of the magnitude of the Cultural Revolution has the responsibility to document and expose them. When crimes are not exposed, criminals are not punished, and more crimes are committed. If we ignore yesterday's tragedy, we risk living in it tomorrow. The change in attitude toward Mao and the Cultural Revolution by the Chinese government and some Chinese people in the past few decades had proven that when victims and witnesses are silent, criminals are covering up their crimes. Father's story and the story of my family belong to history and need to be documented.

To tell Father's story, I had to find the answers to the many questions that I'd had for decades: Why was Father, who was working on a crucial project for China, killed? There were only six months from his last visit back to Beijing to his death. What had happened in those six months? Why would the military hate Father so much? It was incomprehensible that humans would commit such a horrendous crime against another human. Who were the murderers, and what had happened to them?

Finding the truth surrounding Father's death was not an easy task. Chinese nuclear weapons research was a secret in China. For decades, no one had ever told the stories behind the mushroom clouds.

In the years immediately after Mao's death, the government allowed people to expose certain crimes during the Cultural Revolution. It helped to legitimize the new regime after the arrest of Mao's wife. However, once the new government's control grew firm, especially after the 1989 Tiananmen Square massacre, it put a lid on the media as well as the public. Reflection on the Cultural Revolution was discouraged, and public commemoration at anniversaries was forbidden. In the name of harmony and stability, the crimes during the Cultural Revolution were swept under the rug. Voices of anger were muffled.

Despite the difficulties, some individuals—Father's students, friends, colleagues, colleagues' spouses, and complete strangers—took every opportunity to tell Father's story to the public, although many times, they had to use the word "rebels" when referring to the military men to avoid being silenced. From books, articles, government documents, and verbal accounts of the victims of the military brutality, I was able to piece together the sequence of events that led to Father's death.

The research brought me back in time to the peak of the Cultural Revolution. Powerlessly, I watched Father fall into his demise.

CHAPTER SIXTEEN

After the successful detonation of China's first hydrogen bomb in 1967, the people at Factory 221 were given a project for the Chinese Navy. Under the order of the Martial Law Enforcement Committee, the researchers and workers only worked three days a week on nuclear weapons research and production, and the other three days a week, they were made to participate in the Cultural Revolution.

Although Father was still the director of the Second Production Division, in reality, he could not make any decisions without approval from the military men, who had no knowledge about nuclear weapons research. Some of Father's colleagues recalled later that they couldn't even have a small meeting to discuss research-related issues without the military men's permission. Most of the time, the military men would forbid these kinds of meetings. Father's hands were tied, but his responsibilities to lead the research and production for his division were not lightened.

At a kickoff meeting for the navy project, Father told the people in his division that the project would be the most difficult task the division had ever undertaken. They were asked to research and produce new high explosives, small in volume but high in energy.

As the political movement progressed, the military sent some researchers into confinement to be interrogated as class enemies, and other researchers had to shoulder extra work left by the imprisoned. With a reduced workforce and only half of the time left for research and production, many researchers had to work on Sundays.

Most worrisome was that the safety rules and precautions, which had been established over the years and proven to be life-saving for the people in the Second Production Division, were compromised or even abandoned, not only because of the pressure to produce new explosives quickly and the shortage of manpower, but mainly because the military men considered the rules "the bourgeoisie's rules that constrain revolutionary masses' hands and feet." Under the military's orders, routine tests and maintenance of tools and equipment were skipped, safety procedures to conduct experiments were compromised to speed up progress, and thorough analysis of new materials was omitted before experiments. Disasters were waiting to happen.

An accidental explosion shook the division during one experiment. While the wounded researcher was still lying in the hospital, another explosion occurred: a detonator exploded in someone's hand.

The military organized a post-accident meeting, which Father was absent from because, at this time, the military men had taken him away from day-to-day operations to write his confessions. They had scheduled a meeting for him to make a public speech of self-criticism. It seemed that once he publicly criticized his bourgeois viewpoints as a result of growing up in a non-proletarian family and receiving an education from the pre-communist era, he would be able to go back to work.

Ku, the head of the Martial Law Enforcement Committee in the Second Production Division and also a division commander in the Chinese military, attended the post-accident meeting. In the meeting, the researchers suggested that compromising safety procedures was the reason for the explosions and asked for research to be halted for a week to catch any potential safety hazards. However, Ku was infuriated and pointed out that the accidents were not a technical problem; instead, they reflected a class struggle in the division. The request to halt the research was denied.

After gaining power in China, to strengthen its grip over the people and deflect anger away from itself, the government provoked hatred among the Chinese people because a divided people is the easiest to control. The party turned uneducated people against educated people. The uneducated were said to be the most revolutionary, and the educated counter-revolutionary. The popular saying at the time was: "The more knowledge one possesses, the more reactionary one becomes." Mao said on more than one occasion, "The more books they [the educated] read, the more stupid they get." As a result of the communists' people-dividing propaganda of class hatred, upon entering Factory 221, the military men, who were mostly uneducated, considered themselves the trusted watchdogs of the government, whose job was to prevent the "stinky intellectuals" from sabotaging the important mission.

Things went from bad to worse. In addition to the accidents, experimental tests of a neutron initiator didn't release enough neutrons. The tests failed three times in a row.

When the scientists tried to explain to the military men the difficulties of the experiments from a technological point of view, a military man barked, "Technology, technology! Are you trying to scare us with technology? Three failures in a row. Let me ask you: how many times has this happened before?"

The answer was never.

The military man yelled, "Why did all failures happen after we entered Factory 221? Why did all failures happen during the Purifying Class Ranks Movement? And why did some people predict the failures even before the tests?"

The answer was obvious. Anyone with the ability to think critically should have understood that the failures occurred because the military-led political movement had interfered with the scientists' work. However, the military men determined that the scientists and researchers had sabotaged the experiment to smear their glorious image. It enraged them, and more people were locked up.

Although I had never met these military men, somehow, when I read Father's former colleagues' recollections, I could almost see the soldiers' angry faces. During the Cultural

Revolution, I had seen similar faces on the Red Guards who had tormented the university officials, and I had seen them on the revolutionaries at the mass rallies when they'd claimed, "I am a Big Old Rough and proud of it!" Their eyes had been closed and their mouths open. Spit had flown from their lips, and veins had bulged in their temples. They had been willing to harm or even kill their fellow human beings without any hesitation or remorse because they had been told that they were right. Ignorance and blind faith are a deadly combination.

The reality in China didn't allow the military to lock up everyone at Factory 221, though.

The year was 1969, and military conflicts had broken out between the Soviet Union and China at the border. The Chinese leaders wanted to flex their military muscles to the world. Under pressure from the State Council and the Second Ministry of Machinery Industry to accelerate the navy project, the Martial Law Enforcement Committee at Factory 221 halted their witch hunt and allowed the researchers to go back to work.

"If anything goes wrong again," a military official warned, "people need to watch out: the old debts and the new debts will be collected at the same time." The researchers were slaves with fancy titles and worked with the sword of Damocles suspended over their heads. Any failures, accidents, or slowdowns in the progress of the navy project could lead to imprisonment, torture, or even death. For Father and his colleagues, the danger was imminent, and there was no way out.

Deep in the fall of 1969, the sword dangling over the heads of the researchers fell.

An enormous accidental explosion flattened an entire building in the Second Production Division, blowing a few people into pieces. The unprecedented event, along with two other incidents in other divisions, triggered a massive witch hunt.

After the latest explosion, the military representatives in charge at Factory 221 refused to organize any investigations to find the cause of the deadly accident because they had already decided that it was a political event. "What accident?" a military official said. "It was the result of an attack from the counter-revolutionaries. Whoever tries to say this is an accident is trying to cover up class struggle."

With no investigations into the cause of the explosion, the researchers would continue to work in highly dangerous conditions, and more deaths were inevitable.

At this point, Father, who was supposed to take orders from the military men, stepped forward and called a meeting against the military's will. He wanted the cause of the accidents investigated and safety measures reinstated. Already on the verge of being persecuted, he put himself in the military's crosshairs. Calling the meeting was against his cautious nature, but he did it because he had no choice; his colleagues were dying, and people's lives were on the line.

At the meeting, the cause of the accidental explosion was suspected to be malfunctioning equipment used to handle the explosives. Before the accident, the safety inspector of the division had raised concerns and suggested major maintenance on the equipment, but the military had rejected her requests. At the post-accident meeting, Father and another official, who was in charge of safety, requested that all equipment and instruments be thoroughly examined and tested, hoping this would save lives. Father's action to call the meeting angered the military men. They refused to attend the meeting and would use it against Father later.

When I read about the meeting, I knew that Father's fate was sealed.

In China, no differing voices were allowed. To survive was to be silent. Disobeying the government and its military was suicidal. However, knowing Father, I didn't see that he had any other choice.

The Chinese government considered the original Martial Law Enforcement Committee to be too lenient on the researchers and sent in more military men in the form of a workgroup to investigate the "counter-revolutionary cases," including the accidental explosions at the Second Production Division. The heads of the workgroup were two high-ranking military officials: a unit deputy commander of the Chinese Air Force and a navy deputy commander.

While the mission of the original Martial Law Enforcement Committee had been to prevent potential enemies from sabotaging the nuclear weapons program, the military workgroup was there to catch those enemies.

Bloodshed at Factory 221 began.

The military workgroup divided the people at Factory 221 into three groups. One group continued to work in Qinghai, and one group was sent to the new Sichuan Nuclear

Weapons Research Base. The third group was to be sent to a Henan cadre school, where they would be doing physical labor. Surprisingly, most of the key researchers' names were on the cadre school list. At the time, no one except for the military men knew that the third list was a death list. The people on that list were about to be sent to a torture camp set up by the Chinese military, the red devils. Father was on that list.

When I pieced together enough information to figure out the timeline, I realized that on his last trip to Beijing, when Father had told us that he would be going to a cadre school soon, the explosions had already happened, the military workgroup had already been put in place, and Father was about to be sent to the torture camp, but he'd hidden it all from us.

My heart ached when I thought how ignorant I had been about the bleak situation Father was in when he'd visited us the last time. I understood why he'd rushed home. He must have sensed the danger and wanted to see us. When we'd sat on the peaceful lake of the Summer Palace, I hadn't known that danger was lurking and the devil would take Father away from us forever.

After Father had gone back to Qinghai from his last trip to Beijing, the military herded people on the cadre school list to a vacant military camp in Duoba, a place not far from Xining, the capital of Qinghai.

It was sheer terror from then on.

The new military men were said to be the soldiers from the nuclear weapons test base in the Xinjiang Autonomous

Region. They were at the end of their service in the military and ready to be turned into civilians. While they still had their military uniforms on, the red stars on their caps and red collar tabs had been removed. The people at the nuclear weapons research base called the newcomers "secondary representatives" and called the military men who had come before them and worn red stars and collar tabs "military representatives."

Armed and under the military's control, the secondary representatives were in Duoba to do the dirty work of beating up and torturing people. Fed a steady diet of Marxist class hatred by government propaganda their whole lives, the military men were non-discriminative regarding whom they would beat: men or women, sick or healthy. The results of their barbaric acts were broken limbs, nervous breakdowns, and deaths.

It was inconceivable that a government would use its military against its own people, but fear and hatred were the communists' most effective weapons. The decades-long communist rule would not have existed without its military.

One article I found online, which was purportedly a document written by the Beijing Middle-Level People's Court in 1983—seven years after the end of the Cultural Revolution—stated,

> *Between November 1969 and November 1971,*
> *the military workgroup set up 40 illegal prisons*
> *and manufactured more than 200 handcuffs*
> *for torturing, and as a result, more than 4,000*

> *officials, scientific and technical personnel, and workers at Factory 221 and Region 902 (Sichuan Nuclear Weapons Research Bases) of the Ninth Academy were illegally interrogated in isolation or imprisoned. More than 300 people were disabled as the result of persecution. More than 50 people were beaten to death or died from persecution.*[1]

Of course, the document blamed it all on the "Lin Biao, Jiang Qing counter-revolutionary clique," omitting Mao and the government's role in the crime.

I couldn't find any evidence showing that it was Lin Biao or Jiang Qing who had sent the military men to Factory 221. According to a book published in 1987, 11 years after the Cultural Revolution had ended, by the Ministry of Nuclear Industry, *Nuclear Industry of Contemporary China*, it was Mao, Zhou, and other Chinese leaders who had ordered martial law for the nuclear weapons program between 1967 and 1973. Lin Biao and Jiang Qing's names were not mentioned. I suspected that Lin Biao was among the leaders who had ordered martial law, but he was not given credit for it because ordering martial law was considered a good measure, and Lin was considered an enemy of the state who didn't deserve the credit. And most likely, Jiang had not been in the position to give the order.

Clearly, Mao and other Chinese leaders were all part of putting Factory 221 under full military control. The same

---

1 Translated by Ying Qian

book stated that in 1968, it was Mao who had ordered the military to help with the navy's nuclear submarine program. Whether Lin Biao was involved or not, it would have been impossible to send the military to a critical and sensitive place like Factory 221 without Mao's order, and it would have been impossible to carry out Mao's order without help from his right-hand man, Zhou Enlai, the premier of China.

Father's final days came in March of 1970 when the military men locked him up alone in a house in a courtyard. Separating him from the rowhouses in which other researchers were confined was a courtyard that housed five military officials.

It was just a few days after Father's 48th birthday. Although it was springtime, it was still cold on the plateau; birds were not singing, and the grass was still brown. The very next day, in a meeting, his arrest was announced to the researchers. From that day on, day and night, people could hear bone-chilling screams as he underwent the military's interrogation.

In the past, as much as I tried not to think about Father, I couldn't help but fantasize about a different outcome: What if he'd admitted his "crime"? What if he hadn't gone back to Qinghai after his vacation in Beijing? As I gathered information, it became apparent that Father's demise was destined. No one could have survived Mao's China with his integrity intact, and Father was a man of integrity.

Before the interrogation started, the barbaric and ignorant military men had already decided that Father was the "black hand" behind the explosions. "Why did he call the post-accident meeting?" the military men had questioned at one meeting that Father hadn't been allowed to attend. "Why were there many people in the meeting from the university where he used to teach? Why did he tell people not to panic in the meeting? Was he sending a signal to his fellow counter-revolutionaries with his speech?" Father's acts of kindness—giving money to people in need or purchasing toothbrushes and toothpaste for new colleagues from poor families—were used as evidence to prove that he was a Kuomintang spy who was recruiting new agents.

The military wanted Father to admit that he had ordered his students to carry out the explosions to derail the navy project. When torture couldn't make Father comply, the military men were frustrated and humiliated. A little more than one month after Father was arrested, they told other researchers who were also under interrogation, "Qian Jin has already confessed. We will have a 10,000-people rally where he will be giving a public confession to admit his crimes. Our workgroup leaders will release him on the spot, and he will walk away a free man. If you confess, you will be free, too."

At the same time, the military turned up the intensity of interrogation on Father. Not only did the leaders of the workgroup want him to confess, but the secondary representatives who were doing the interrogation also needed him to admit his and his students' "crimes." His confession would make them heroes. Sadly, Mao's followers' cruelty matched the tyrant's.

One horrific scene at the Duoba military camp was described by Father's colleague Lu, who was also under interrogation. One day, when he and the soldier watching him were waiting outside the interrogation room, he was able to see and hear as Father was being interrogated by a few military men.

"Qian Jin!" an interrogator barked. It was a warning and a threat. It meant a savage beating would follow. Father retreated, putting his back against a wall. It was obvious to Lu that Father was having difficulty moving. Lu, who had been beaten himself, knew all too well that the victim of beatings would try to have his back against a wall so that he would not be attacked from all sides. The beating lasted a few minutes.

"Were you sabotaging the research? Did you order your students to cause the explosions?" a military man yelled.

"No," Father said, struggling to stand up.

"Other people have already confessed and said that you work for the Kuomintang Northwestern Army," one interrogator said. "If you cooperate and make a public confession, you will be freed on the spot. You would be a fool to try to be a hero. No one knows what happened here. We can say whatever we want. As a matter of fact, we already told all your colleagues that you have confessed. It makes no sense for you to deny it."

"I can't admit to things that I didn't do," Father said. He was having difficulty breathing.

"Are you saying you are not working for the Kuomintang?"

"I am not working for the Kuomintang."

"Do you dare to write down what you just said: you are not a Kuomintang spy?"

"Give me a piece of paper and a pen," Father said.

When a piece of paper and a pen were laid on the table, Father did not hesitate. He struggled to move toward the table.

The interrogators surrounded Father like a pack of wolves cornering prey. One of them put his hand on the paper and said, "This is the last chance that the party and people give to you. Once it is on the paper, it means you refuse our help. We will not work with you anymore. You should know the consequences."

I don't know what went through Father's mind. He had to know that once he wrote down the statement claiming his innocence, it would bring more beating, torture, and eventually death. It meant that he would never see his wife, his children, and his parents again. Father ignored the interrogators and bent his body. He was trying to sit on a stool in front of the table and write down the truth. Just as he was about to sit down, one of the military men made a last desperate attempt to stop Father and kicked away the stool, and Father fell on the floor.

Lu was pushed away by the military man who was escorting him. As he walked away, he could hear the sound of beating and screams from behind him. That was the last time that anyone except the military men saw Father alive. Unable to defeat Father, the Chinese military destroyed him.

Tears rolled down my face when I read Lu's account. I believed every word, especially the details about how Father had intended to sit down and write the truth. Severely beaten and with his life in danger, Father wouldn't have just scribbled a few words. That was the man I knew. A man of integrity, he lived every minute of his life with dignity and decency.

Strangely, I realized that it was not the first time I had learned the story, especially the details of how Father had tried to sit down and write and how the military man had kicked his stool away. When I was 13 or 14 years old, I'd learned it either from Mother's notes or from Father's students who'd visited us. Somehow, I had completely forgotten it. Our memory has a mysterious way of protecting us.

The most difficult day came when I read an article by someone with the pen name "Lao Zhe" on a popular Chinese-language website, *Xin Lang*, where people posted their blogs publicly. In 2007, Lao Zhe documented the suffering Father and his colleagues had endured at a torture camp set up by the Chinese military. I assume Lao Zhe had been one of Father's colleagues.

"It was another cold winter day at the end of 1969," Lao Zhe started. "The wind was howling down from the north. A steam engine train was breathing heavily on the bare land of the Qinghai plateau. The train crawled along, dragging a series of freight train boxcars."

The train didn't haul freight, though, according to Lao Zhe. Instead, the windowless, seatless boxcars carried people and their baggage. They were Factory 221 employees—scientists, engineers, technicians, and workers. The military men who were leading the political movement at Factory 221 had told them that they were being sent down to the Zhumadian cadre school in Henan province to be "steeled by physical labor." The people were anxious. For more than half a year, many of them had endured endless interrogations, forced confessions, and persecution rallies under the military. Should they trust the military's words now? Were they really leaving the nightmare behind, or were they heading into even more danger?

Outside the boxcars was the monotone sound of the wheels and wind, while inside was dead silence. There was no laughing and no talking. Only nervous eye contact every now and then revealed a sense of extreme confusion and uneasiness.

On that chilly day when the punishing wind lashed the barren land, inside the dark boxcars and curled up among their belongings, the people from Factory 221 headed into the darkness of the unknown.

Among them was Father.

"Sitting on his baggage with his knees bent," Lao Zhe wrote, "wearing an old blue winter jacket and a winter hat was the nationally renowned high-energy explosives expert, the head of the Second Production Division of Factory 221, Professor Qian Jin. Next to him was his student, Zhao Rong, who was in his thirties..."

According to Lao Zhe, the train didn't reach the cadre

school in Henan. It didn't even leave Qinghai province. When the train stopped and the heavy iron doors opened, the people eagerly breathed in the fresh air and looked outside. There were no people or buildings in sight. The train was on a special-purpose railroad far away from the train station. As their eyes adjusted to the bright sunlight of the plateau, the people inside the boxcars noticed a few dark-green, ten-wheeled military trucks nearby with armed military men standing guard.

As soon as the doors to the boxcars opened, armed soldiers jumped out of the trucks, screaming as they ran toward the train, "Get down! Bring your baggage!" The confused people quickly exited the dark boxcars and put their belongings on the trucks. As they climbed into the trucks under the soldiers' watch, they realized they hadn't escaped the military's grip. The misery continued.

The trucks took the prisoners to a huge military base in a small town named Duoba, the first stop on Qinghai to Tibet road (Xining-Lhasa). The base used to house a cavalry brigade. It was now empty.

After the newcomers settled in the rowhouses, they were told they were here for a study group and would only be sent to the cadre school afterward. The rules of the Duoba study group were announced: the people in the study group were forbidden to "leave the base, meet friends and family, contact the outside world, communicate with others without permission, and leak information to other people."

The atmosphere intensified. Lao Zhe recalled, "Every

night, listening to the heavy steps of the armed soldiers patrolling back and forth, the people in the rowhouses had a heavy heart as if a big rock were weighing on it."

Lao Zhe identified the armed soldiers as "a group of soldiers who had just come from Xinjiang and joined the study group as the primary force in the movement." I believe those were the "secondary representatives" I'd heard about from some of Father's colleagues. The soldiers had worked at the Xinjiang nuclear weapons test base. They used to admire the people at Factory 221. "Look at the people in blue winter coats who sit right before the stage," they would tell their fellow soldiers during celebration rallies after a successful detonation of the bomb. "They are the people who made the bomb that we tested."

In Duoba, the military men converted some rowhouses into prisons. They sealed the back window high above the floor with lumber and covered the front window with newspapers from the outside. It was dark inside. There was one light bulb hanging from the ceiling. The military men moved the light switch to the outside. In the frigid winter of the great Northwest, the wind was bone-chillingly cold. The inmates had no heat and no beds. Each was allowed only a pile of hay and a blanket, washbasin, and mug. The interrogators were divided into two shifts to interrogate, and inmates were not allowed to have any rest.

Father's student Zhao Rong was one of the prisoners, and in his blog, Lao Zhe documented Zhao Rong's experience in the hands of the military. I believe that "Lao Zhe" was, in fact, Zhao Rong.

On a quiet evening, the screaming of the interrogators and the howling of someone being tortured in the interrogation room could be heard. The howling sounded like the person's organs were being ripped open. Zhao Rong's interrogation continued for more than 50 hours. He felt his surroundings spinning and shaking. Everything in his vision became dark yellow. Eventually, it was all dark, and Zhao Rong fell to the floor.

Next was another round of beating with a high-pressure hose, fists, and feet. But he could not feel anything except that his heart was burning. Zhao Rong was so thirsty that if he'd had a bucket of water in front of him, he would have been able to drink it in one gulp. When the interrogators finally got tired, they dragged Zhao Rong back to his confinement cell and dumped him on a pile of hay.

As I read Lao Zhe's blog, I was shaking. Many times, I had to stop because I couldn't breathe. The Chinese soldiers under the communists were indeed animals in uniforms. As hard as it was, I forced myself to continue reading. It was from Lao Zhe's blog that I learned the details of Father's arrest.

That morning, the military men came to the rowhouses where the study group members were staying and searched every dresser, every drawer, and "even people's bodies, including women and children," as Lao Zhe noted in his blog. After the search and even before people had the time to organize their rooms, the chilling sound of a whistle pierced the still air; an emergency meeting had been called. Father, Zhao Rong, and no more than 100 others ran toward a big athletic field. There, they stood in a row with their backs against the houses and their faces toward the field. On their left, right, and front were soldiers carrying rifles, which they pointed forward.

The military men then took the people into an old, large storage room with a stage at the front.

At the most prominent spot on the stage stood two military officials, one in army uniform and the other air force. The people sat quietly on little stools with their heads lowered, wondering what would happen that day.

The host announced the meeting had begun. The army official (a current division commander) screamed, "A small group of class enemies is hiding very deep in our study group; they are active counter-revolutionaries and spies! We are going to clear them all out!" Then he shouted, "Qian Jin has serious political issues. From now on, he will be imprisoned and interrogated!"

Immediately two large men sitting behind Father stood up. They dragged him out of the room with his arms forced behind him and his head pushed down. When Father was dragged past Zhao Rong, his student could hear the teacher moan. "From that day on," Lao Zhe wrote, "the slim-framed, benevolent-faced, kind, and respected intellectual disappeared from sight."

My heart ached. The article described a scene I had witnessed many times when I'd attended the persecution rallies at the university; only then, it had been the students, not the military men, who had manhandled officials. It pained me to think that when I had been shouting slogans against the university officials, Father had been receiving similar treatment by the military men a thousand miles away in Qinghai.

Lao Zhe also wrote about the last time Zhao Rong saw Father.

That morning, Zhao Rong was escorted to the interrogation room. The snow that had accumulated overnight crunched under his steps. Suddenly, the soldier escorting him shouted, "Stop! Lower your head!"

Zhao Rong was confused. He stopped and lowered his head. From the corner of his eye, he saw Father, whom he hadn't seen for a while, being escorted out of the interrogation room by two interrogators. He was limping badly. Zhao Rong could not believe his eyes. In just a few days, his teacher had become a different person. His hair was uncombed, and the signs of suffering were evident. He was still wearing the old dark-blue winter jacket, only now the jacket was tattered, and cotton was exposed in many spots. This was the result of the whipping. "The teacher and the student passed each other unexpectedly at this time and this moment," Lao Zhe wrote. "No one said a word. But their eye contact revealed more than words could tell. Who could have known that this brief meeting would be the last time the teacher and the student saw each other?"

I could sense the profound sadness in Lao Zhe's words, though he was describing a scene from more than 30 years before. Taking a deep breath, I continued reading. Lao Zhe described another scene:

> *In the interrogation room, four large men surrounded Qian Jin again. They were trying to force him to admit that he was a Kuomintang general army commander leading a Northwestern Underground Advance Army and that his students were the key army members. Qian Jin, of course, refused firmly. The thugs were frustrated. After another round of beating, Qian Jin, who was almost 50 years old, could not stand anymore. He had to squat. A thug wearing a big-toed leather boot kicked Qian Jin in his lower abdomen. Qian Jin moaned and fell. He trembled in pain and could not move. The thugs didn't stop beating. They were yelling, "Are you pretending to be dead?" Qian Jin didn't respond to the beating. The thugs panicked. Qian Jin held on to a leg of the table with both arms. The thugs attempted to separate his arms and drag him out of the room. But Qian Jin said breathlessly and angrily, "I am not going out. I will die here."[2]*

Tears came down my face. Reading Lao Zhe's blog was the hardest thing I'd ever had to do. I was consumed with anger. Many times, I had to stop because I was afraid I would read something even more graphic. To keep going,

2   Translated by Ying Qian

I had to tell myself that this would be the worst day and I would get through it.

Although I had never read Lao Zhe's blog before, somehow what I read sounded familiar, especially the scene in the interrogation room, where Father refused to be removed from the torture chamber and when he said that he was going to die there. I realized I had already learned about the incident from Father's colleagues in the early 1970s. However, over the past few decades, I'd had no memory of it. Subconsciously, I must have erased the memory because it was too graphic and too painful to remember.

In his blog, Lao Zhe also mentioned the crate that our family received after Father's death.

After Lin Biao's failed coup in 1971, Father's students were released from prison. Although still under the military's control, they were allowed to organize Father's belongings.

Lao Zhe wrote:

> *The respected professor, who had students all over the country, had only left behind two wooden crates. The students opened the crates. They found that one crate was filled with books. The other had simple clothing, a Go game, and a ping-pong paddle; that was all.*
>
> *The tearful students cleaned their beloved teacher's clothes to send them back*

to Beijing. But they saved one shirt with a stain of blood on it. They didn't touch it. They kept it the way it was. It was evidence of what had happened.

Lao Zhe's blog clearly revealed that Father had left two crates, but we'd only received one. The one with books had never reached our family. I couldn't tell what had happened to the letters that we'd sent to Father; Lao Zhe didn't say. The military men must have already confiscated them for evidence. The students had put the bloody shirt, the Go game, and the ping-pong paddle in the wooden crate to be sent back to Beijing, but when Mother had opened it, none of these items had been there. It had to have been the military men who took the bloody shirt out of the crate to cover up the crime. But why did they take the Go game and the ping-pong paddle? My conclusion was that they did it because they could. They could take away Father's life without ever being punished; what was a Go game or a ping-pong paddle?

In conclusion, Lao Zhe wrote:

Qian Jin was sincere, earnest, gracious, and pleasant. On his table was a motto in his own handwriting: "Reflect on my own faults often and never gossip about others' shortcomings."

The diligent scholar, who made a tremendous contribution to modernizing

> *the defense industry for our country, died in great injustice in those "unprecedented years."*

Father had adhered to his motto his whole life. The motto might have reflected his upbringing as a classic gentleman, a grandson of a classic Chinese scholar, and been inspired by the high standards of generations of traditional Chinese intellectuals, but it was also a reflection of an honest man's struggle to maintain his integrity, dignity, and honesty at a time when a dictator and his loyalists forced people to implicate one another.

My father, a brilliant scientist who could have done so much good for mankind, died defending truth and human dignity. A caring husband, he didn't get to grow old with my mother, the love of his life. A loving father, he didn't get to watch his children grow or see his grandchildren.

While it was extremely difficult to read Lao Zhe's article, it gave me insight into Father's state of mind in his last days. Even in the communist movies, in the Kuomintang's prisons, the underground communists were able to leave letters to their loved ones after they died, but Father hadn't left anything behind. The communists had taken everything he had and destroyed it all.

For more than 40 years, as much as I avoided it, I still couldn't help but think about what Father had gone through in the last days of his life, the days in the cold and barren plateau, away from his family and people who loved him. Had he seen through the communists' barbaric nature at the end of his life, or had he still had false hope that the communists would allow him to tell the truth and live?

From Lao Zhe's article, I knew that at the end, Father had been prepared to die. He'd been aware that the military would eventually kill him and lie about his death if he refused to comply. Father had been locked up alone, and no one except his killers knew how he had died. When he had said, "I am going to die here" in the presence of another victim, he had been letting people know that it was the Chinese military that had killed him. He hadn't wanted the crimes to be buried after his death.

After Lin Biao's death, another group of military men, the Central Committee Communication Group, was sent in by the Chinese Communist Party Central Committee to end the bloody Purifying Class Ranks Movement. While the beatings and torture stopped and the people were released, the attempt to bring criminals to justice was forbidden. "No naming names," the new military group warned the victims.

The military Communication Group decided that the criminals who had savagely tortured and killed innocent people were victims themselves. Instead of being sent to prisons, the criminals were well taken care of: the military representatives went back to their original units in the military, and to help the secondary representatives find civilian jobs, the Communication Group formed 17 teams to look for employment for them all over the country. Within six months, the criminals and murderers dissipated throughout the country, becoming civilian workers.

Father's killers walked, and as far as I know, none of

the people who were directly involved in torturing or even killing the victims served time in prison.

Many researchers, technicians, and workers left Factory 221, and many were sent to a new nuclear weapons research base in Sichuan province.

In 1983, seven years after the Cultural Revolution, one of the military leaders of the witch hunt at Factory 221 was sentenced to 15 years in prison.

In 1987, Factory 221 was shut down. The site became a tourist attraction.

The impact of the Cultural Revolution on China, as well as the world, has been profound and long-lasting. The 10 years of the Cultural Revolution were a selection process: the accomplished, the courageous, and the honest died, and the killers lived and were not punished. A people who already lacked spiritual belief discovered that crimes didn't have to be punished as long as they were done for a "noble" cause and by the masses.

I still don't know *who* killed my father, but I know *what* killed him—an egomaniacal dictator who mastered the art of the power struggle perfected by rulers over thousands of years of Chinese history; a people-dividing, hatred-provoking communist ideology that was used as a tool by the dictator to lure and control his followers; a government that took power with violence and maintained it with blood; a stagnant culture that worshiped power and oppressed individuals; and a political environment in which the beast in men was allowed to run wild.

Father's demise was the result of a deadly combination

of a dictator's ruthlessness and the grassroots' cruelty. Mao started and led the Cultural Revolution, but it was the people who were as cruel as Mao who made it as bloody as it was. In the Cultural Revolution, animals came in human form, and ordinary people did extraordinary evil. It was a perfect storm of red terror. In the path of the storm was Father, who refused to bend.

My father, the gentlest person I have ever known, was also the most courageous man I have ever met. A quiet and humble man, he died protecting the truth, human dignity, and the lives of his students. Father didn't set out to be a hero, but in China, telling the truth required a hero's courage.

For decades, I viewed Father as a victim of the brutality of the Chinese Communist Party and its military. Now, I know that Father was not just another helpless victim. Under extremely difficult circumstances, he fought a lonely fight and paid with his life. While complying with the communists might have saved him, Father chose to die. He was courageous, and his courage came from his integrity. He was the same honest man Mother had fallen in love with many years before. He did what he always told us children to do: tell the truth. However, in a dictatorship, telling the truth cost him his life.

In the 20 years of living under the communist regime, he was denied facts, and he did things that he was forced to do for his safety, for the well-being of his family, and for the hope that the regime would correct its "mistakes" and allow its people to live normal lives. He believed his efforts and sacrifices were for his beloved people. But in the end, Father made his last and fatal decision. By choosing death, he severed all ties with the evil regime.

Father is still my role model more than 40 years after his death, but not for the reasons that I used to believe: his achievements in his field, his contribution to the Chinese nuclear weapons program, his self-sacrifice for his country, or the validation he received from the government. He is my role model because of *who he was*, not because of *what he did*. Against an evil dictatorship and its ferocious killing machine, he stood as his own person, honest and brave, with his integrity intact.

My father, my hero.

ACKNOWLEDGMENTS

I want to thank Jessie Dugan for her unwavering support, starting from the early phases of creating the book.

My gratitude goes to Barbara Lee for her thorough and thoughtful review of the manuscript.

I am grateful for Ashley Gibson's help when I needed a fresh eye from a different angle to evaluate my manuscript.

I especially want to thank the developmental editor for this project, Gary Smailes. His to-the-point comments and in-depth analysis elevated the book.

Christine Pingleton has given invaluable assistance in proofreading. Her patience and support are appreciated as much as her knowledge and skills.

My deep gratitude goes to my editor Jefferson from FirstEditing. His thoroughness and professionalism improved the book greatly.

I would like to thank Madeleine Swart, whose editorial skills and expertise as well as her keen eye for detail helped improve the quality of the book.

Finally, I want to thank my loving husband of more than 25 years. Bill is my first reader, editor, and sounding board. Without his patience, support, and sacrifice, this book would not be possible.

CHRONOLOGY

The information below was collected from books, newspapers, the internet, and my own memories. The years listed are when a political movement started. Some political movements lasted beyond a year. Since they ended at different times, depending on the area, the ending years are often not listed.

Pre–Cultural Revolution

1949 The Communist Party took power in China, and the People's Republic of China was proclaimed.

1950 The Land Reform Movement began.[1] Farmland owners were persecuted, and the land was confiscated and divided into small plots and given to peasants by the communist government.

My mother's father was sent to a reform-through-labor camp for 10 years as a punishment for legally owning 10 acres of farmland.

The same year, the Campaign to Suppress Counter-Revolutionaries started. The main targets were Kuomintang agents, former Kuomintang military

---

1 The Land Reform Movement started in 1947 in some communist-controlled areas.

personnel, as well as organizations the government considered a threat.

1951   The Three Antis/Five Antis Campaign began, targeting business owners and purging government employees.

1954   The Public-Private Partnership Movement began. The government confiscated private businesses. Former business owners became workers and received "fixed interest," which stopped in 1966.

1955   The Eliminate Hidden Counter-Revolutionaries Movement took place, purging counter-revolutionaries within the party, the government, and the military.

The Eliminate the Hufeng Counter-Revolutionary Group Movement began, purging dissidents in the literary field.

1957   Moscow agreed to help China develop nuclear weapons.

The Anti-Rightist Campaign started. More than half a million people, the majority of whom were educated, were officially labeled as "rightists" and punished. Many were sent to the Chinese gulags to do hard labor.

1958   The Great Leap Forward Movement started. Farmland was confiscated from the peasants by the government to form people's communes. Taxation and lack of farmhands due to an effort to make steel in "backyard furnaces" caused the "Three Years of Famine" and millions of deaths. Nevertheless,

China's nuclear weapons program charged forward. I was born this year.

1959   As a result of a falling out between Beijing and Moscow, the Soviets began the withdrawal of any forms of help from the Chinese nuclear weapons program. China continued its pursuit of nuclear weapons without further help from the Soviets.

1960   My father was ordered to leave our family and join the nuclear weapons program. He was 37 years old, and I was two.

1962   Conference of the Seven Thousand People. Chairman Liu Shaoqi led an effort to end the famine caused by the Great Leap Forward Movement.

1963   The Four Cleanups Movement, a.k.a. Socialist Education Movement, started. Mao raised the issue of "class struggle" to counter Liu. Mao also warned about the capitalist-roaders within the party.

1964   China tested its first atomic bomb.

Cultural Revolution

1966   The Great Proletarian Cultural Revolution started. The Red Guard Movement began in Beijing and then spread to the whole nation. Police became nonexistent. Many people died a violent death at the hands of the Red Guards.

I was eight.

1967   Mass organizations were formed throughout the nation, and violent fights broke out among them. China detonated its first hydrogen bomb. The Cultural Revolution began in the nuclear weapons facility in Qinghai, where my father worked.

1968   The Purifying Class Ranks Movement began. Liberation Army Mao Zedong Thought Propaganda Teams as well as Workers Mao Zedong Thought Propaganda Teams were formed and sent to schools and government entities to lead the movement. The military hand-picked Mao's loyalists to form revolutionary committees to replace former leadership throughout the nation. My mother was persecuted as a historical counter-revolutionary and sentenced to hard labor for years.

The same year, the City Youth Sent-Down Movement began. City youth were sent to remote areas to do farmwork and be re-educated by peasants. My oldest brother, aged 18, was among them.

1969   Former chairman of China Liu Shaoqi died in confinement. Lin Biao was recognized by the party as Mao's "closest comrade-in-arms and successor." My other brother was sent away to do farmwork. He was 16.

1970   My father was killed at the Qinghai nuclear weapons facility by the military. He was 48. I was 12.

The One Strike–Three Anti Campaign started, during which many people were arrested and executed.

1971   The government announced that Lin Biao, his wife, his son, and members of his staff attempted to flee to the Soviet Union to seek asylum after a failed coup. Their plane crashed in Mongolia, killing all on board.

1972   The Criticize Lin (Biao) Rectification Movement began.

1973   Former party official Deng Xiaoping was brought back to Beijing from exile to focus on reconstructing the Chinese economy.

1974   The Criticize Lin and Criticize Confucius Movement began. In schools, the Against the Tide Movement was launched against teachers.

1975   Mao was dissatisfied with Deng, and Deng was made to draw up a series of self-criticisms.

1976   The Criticize Deng and Oppose the Rehabilitation
        of Right-leaning Elements Campaign started early
        in the year.
        Mao died. His wife, Jiang Qing, was arrested. The
        Cultural Revolution ended.
        I graduated from high school.

www.ingramcontent.com/pod-product-compliance
Lightning Source LLC
Chambersburg PA
CBHW021240060726
47590CB00005B/1829